winter
recipe collection
volume 2
by **Sainsbury's**

A collection of 100 more warming winter dishes

welcome...

Our first book of winter recipes went down a storm, so we've put our heads together to come up with even more mouthwatering ideas for keeping the family well-fed and happy over the winter months. From delicious soups that are a meal in themselves to perfect pies, slow-cooked casseroles, wonderful wintry puds and inspiration for all those seasonal special occasions, our selection of recipes will help to inspire you to create meals you'll want to make over and over again. Using the very best seasonal ingredients, along with plenty of handy storecupboard staples, all of the recipes have been tried, tested and tasted, so you can be confident they'll work first time – and every time. Whether you're after ideas for everyday mealtimes or a special family celebration, you'll find what you're after in our second winter collection.

Happy cooking!

contents

We've added icons to make everything as clear as possible:

 Suitable for vegetarians

 Recipes containing 1 or more of your 5-a-day, to help you plan for healthier eating. Try to eat at least 5 different portions of fruit and veg a day. Fresh, frozen, dried, canned and juice all count.

For an explanation of the nutritional breakdown of each recipe featured, please turn to p193. Nutrition is calculated using each recipe's ingredients list only and does not include any sides, accompaniments or other serving suggestions mentioned in the method unless otherwise stated.

soups

Speedy chicken broth	8
Savoury drop scones	8
Leek, chicken & pearl barley soup	10
Ham & potato soup	12
Pancetta, rosemary & red lentil soup	14
Mulligatawny	16
Lamb & chickpea soup	18
Goats' cheese croutons	18
Classic fish soup	20
Baby leaf spinach soup with salmon	22
Melba toasts	22
Spiced parsnip soup with chestnuts	24
Borscht	26

Speedy chicken broth

A quick version of a classic recipe, this is on the table in just 30 mins

1.5 litres chicken stock, made with 1 stock cube
Few sprigs of fresh rosemary
400g pack British mini chicken fillets
by Sainsbury's
1 large carrot, peeled and sliced
100g mange tout, finely sliced

150g frozen peas
100g bag baby leaf spinach by Sainsbury's
Juice and zest of 1 lemon
Small handful fresh flat-leaf parsley
leaves, chopped
Crusty bread, to serve

1 Pour the stock into a large pan, add the rosemary sprigs and bring to a simmer.
   Add the chicken and carrots, and poach the chicken for 8 mins, until cooked
   through with no pink remaining. Remove the chicken and rosemary sprigs with a
   slotted spoon and set aside. Once cool enough to handle, cut the chicken into
   bite-size pieces. Discard the rosemary.

2 Add the mange tout and peas to the hot stock and cook for 5-6 mins, then stir
   in the spinach and cook for a further 1 min. Stir in the lemon juice and return the
   chicken to the pan and heat through until piping hot.

3 Serve garnished with the lemon zest and chopped parsley alongside chunks of
   the crusty bread.

Per serving: 1894kJ/447kcal (22%), 4g fat (6%), 1.1g saturates (6%),
5g sugars (6%), 2.25g salt (38%)

Savoury drop scones Ⓥ

Sift 125g self-raising flour and 1 tsp baking powder
into a bowl. Season to taste. Whisk in 1 beaten egg
and 2 tbsp semi-skimmed milk (taken from 125ml).
Whisk in the rest of the milk to form a smooth batter,
then add 1 tbsp fresh thyme leaves. Drop spoonfuls
into a hot, lightly greased frying pan. Cook for 3 mins,
turning once - you will need to do this in batches.

Makes 18 Prep time: 10 mins Cook time: 12 mins
Per scone: 137kJ/32kcal (2%), <0.5g fat (<1%),
0.2g saturates (1%), 0.6g sugars (1%), 0.08g salt (1%)

Leek, chicken & pearl barley soup

This hearty thickened chicken broth full of comforting flavours will warm your bones on a chilly evening

2 whole chicken legs by Sainsbury's
1 litre chicken stock, made with 1 stock cube
1 small onion, chopped
1 carrot, chopped
1 stick celery, trimmed and chopped
A few black peppercorns

1 fresh bay leaf
100g pearl barley
3 leeks, trimmed and sliced
3 tbsp double cream, to serve
Small handful fresh flat-leaf parsley, leaves picked and chopped

1   Put the chicken legs in a medium pan, then add the stock, onion, carrot, celery, peppercorns, bay leaf and 650ml cold water. Bring to the boil and simmer for 20 mins until cooked through with no pink remaining, partially covered.

2   Meanwhile, cook the pearl barley: drain and rinse in cold water, tip into a pan and cover with cold water, then bring to the boil and simmer for 30 mins.

3   Strain the stock from the chicken, discarding the vegetables, bay leaf and peppercorns, and set aside the chicken. Pour the stock into a clean pan, add the cooked drained barley and simmer for 15 mins. Add the leeks and simmer for a further 15 mins.

4   Shred the chicken, discarding the skin and bones, and add to the pan. Heat through until piping hot. Season to taste and stir in the cream and parsley just before ladling into warm bowls.

Per serving: 1351kJ/324kcal (16%), 18.2g fat (26%), 35g saturates (6.9%), 7.6g sugars (8%), 1.25g salt (21%)

Cook's tip
Make this soup even heartier by cooking with country soup mix – a mix of lentils, pulses and barley.

SERVES 4
PREP TIME
20 mins, plus
overnight soaking
and cooling
COOK TIME 1 hour –
1 hour 10 mins

Ham & potato soup

Simple but sensational, this chunky soup is filling and flavoursome

750g unsmoked gammon joint by
Sainsbury's, soaked overnight in cold water
1 tbsp olive oil
1 onion, chopped
3 sticks celery, trimmed and chopped
2 large potatoes, peeled and diced

3 cloves garlic, finely sliced
Small handful fresh flat-leaf parsley
leaves, roughly chopped, plus extra
leaves to garnish
200ml single cream

1   Drain and rinse the soaked gammon joint and put it in a large pan or stock pot.
    Cover with cold water, bring to the boil and simmer, partially covered, for
    45 mins, until tender. Remove from the heat and leave to cool in the liquid.
    Transfer the gammon to a board and strain the gammon stock through a sieve
    into a large bowl. Reserve 1 litre of the stock for making the soup, then shred
    250g of the meat into bite-size chunks (see cook's tip). Taste the stock and,
    if it's too salty, dilute with water.

2   Heat the oil in a large heavy-based pan and add the onion, celery and potatoes.
    Cook over a medium heat for 10-12 mins until tender. Stir through the garlic and
    cook for a further 1 min.

3   Return the reserved stock to the pan and bring to the boil. Continue to simmer
    for 10-12 mins, until the potatoes are tender. Stir in the torn meat with the
    chopped parsley and cream. Garnish with the extra parsley leaves and serve
    seasoned with freshly ground black pepper.

Per serving: 1642kJ/393kcal (20%), 19.7g fat (28%), 8.5g saturates (43%),
5.6g sugars (6%), 2.01g salt (34%)

Cook's tip
You will have plenty of gammon leftover. It's delicious
served cold, in sandwiches with sweet pickle, or you
could stir it through another soup.

Pancetta, rosemary & red lentil soup

Smoky pancetta and earthy rosemary make a great pairing, while the red lentils break down during cooking for a hearty consistency

2 tbsp olive oil
½ x 160g pack Italian cubetti di pancetta
with herbs by Sainsbury's
1 onion, roughly chopped
2 sticks celery, trimmed and roughly chopped
3 cloves garlic, finely chopped
1 carrot, peeled and roughly chopped
175g dried red lentils

2 tbsp tomato purée
3 sprigs fresh rosemary
1 litre vegetable stock, made with 1 stock cube
1-2 slices of crusty white bread, crusts
removed and discarded and bread cut
into small croutons
4 tbsp crème fraîche

1   Heat 1 tbsp of the oil in a large heavy-based pan over a medium heat. Add the pancetta, onion and celery and fry for 4-5 mins until the pancetta is golden. Stir through the chopped garlic and carrot, and cook for a further 1 min.

2   Put the lentils in a sieve and rinse under cold running water until the water runs clear. Add the lentils to the pan along with the tomato purée and rosemary, and mix well.

3   Pour in the stock, bring to the boil, then simmer for 20-25 mins, until the lentils and vegetables are tender. Remove the rosemary sprigs from the soup and discard. Season to taste with freshly ground black pepper, remove from the heat and allow to cool slightly. Use a hand blender to blend the soup until smooth.

4   Meanwhile, make the croutons. Preheat the oven to 200ºC, fan 180ºC, gas 6. Toss the bread in the remaining olive oil and transfer to a baking sheet. Bake for 10 mins, tossing half way through until crisp and golden.

5   Serve the soup with a swirl of crème fraîche and a scattering of croutons.

Per serving: 1283kJ/308kcal (15%), 17.8g fat (25%), 6.9g saturates (35%), 7.4g sugars (8%), 1.84g salt (31%)

SERVES 4
PREP TIME 15 mins
COOK TIME 35 mins

Mulligatawny

This richly flavoured soup spiced with curry paste is a great dish for using up leftover roast beef

1 tbsp vegetable oil

1 onion, chopped

1 carrot, peeled and diced

2 sticks celery, trimmed and diced

2 tbsp plain flour

2 tbsp balti curry paste by Sainsbury's

85g basmati rice

300g leftover roast beef, shredded or diced (see cook's tip, below)

1 litre chicken stock, made with 1 stock cube

390g carton Italian chopped tomatoes by Sainsbury's

1 eating apple, peeled, cored and grated

Small handful fresh coriander leaves, to garnish

1   Heat the oil in a large pan over a low heat. Add the onion, carrot and celery, and sweat the vegetables for about 10 mins, until soft and the onion and celery are translucent. Stir through the plain flour and curry paste, and cook for a further 1 min. Stir through the rice and mix well.

2   Add the beef to the pan with the stock and tomatoes, and simmer for 15 mins, until the rice is tender and the beef is piping hot. Stir in the grated apple and heat through for 2-3 mins.

3   Divide between bowls and serve garnished with the coriander.

Per serving: 1584kJ/377kcal (19%), 13.1g fat (19%), 4.5g saturates (23%), 10.7g sugars (12%), 1.45g salt (24%)

Cook's tip

If you do not have any leftover beef for this recipe, heat 1 tbsp vegetable oil in a frying pan and sear a 275g piece of steak for 2-3 mins each side. Remove from the pan and rest for 10 mins before slicing and adding to the soup pot in step 2.

Lamb & chickpea soup

Our version of the popular, fragrant Moroccan soup *harira* is super easy to prepare and cook

1 tbsp olive oil, plus extra if needed

250g pack 20% fat lamb mince by Sainsbury's

1 onion, roughly chopped

2 cloves garlic, thinly sliced

1 tsp ground cinnamon

1 tsp ground cumin

2 tbsp tomato purée

390g carton chopped tomatoes by Sainsbury's

450ml hot lamb stock, made with 1 stock cube

410g tin chickpeas, drained and rinsed

1 courgette, trimmed and diced

Zest and juice of ½ lemon

Fresh coriander leaves, to garnish

1   Heat the olive oil in a heavy-based pan and fry the lamb mince until brown and starting to crisp. Using a slotted spoon, remove from the pan and set aside.

2   Add a little more oil to the pan if needed then add the onion and garlic. Fry for 3-4 mins, over a medium heat, until softened. Stir through the cinnamon, cumin and tomato purée, and cook for 2-3 mins. Return the lamb mince to the pan with the chopped tomatoes, stock and chickpeas. Simmer for 20-25 mins.

3   Add the courgette and cook for 3 mins until the courgette is just tender. Add the lemon juice and mix well. Ladle into 4 bowls and serve garnished with the lemon zest and coriander leaves, with a goats' cheese crouton on the side (see below).

Per serving without croutons: 1350kJ/323kcal (16%), 16.7g fat (24%), 6.8g saturates (34%), 7.7g sugars (9%), 0.51g salt (9%)

Goats' cheese croutons ⓥ

Preheat the grill to high and toast 4 thick slices French baguette on one side. Transfer to a board and brush the untoasted side with olive oil. Crumble over 80g goats' cheese and dust with a little smoked paprika. Return to the grill and cook for 2 mins until the goats' cheese has just started to brown.

Makes 4 Prep time: 5 mins Cook time: 5-10 mins
Per crouton: 366kJ/89kcal (5%), 8.2g fat (12%), 4g saturates (20%), <0.5g sugars (<1%), 0.32g salt (5%)

Classic fish soup

Simple but delicious, this easy fish soup is great to serve as a starter if you have friends coming over for dinner

2 tbsp olive oil
1 large onion, finely chopped
2 cloves garlic, chopped
2 sticks celery, trimmed and finely sliced
Zest and juice of 1 orange
Pinch of cayenne pepper
390g carton Italian chopped tomatoes by Sainsbury's
750ml hot fish stock, made with 1 stock cube

240g pack boneless Scottish salmon fillets by Sainsbury's, cut into chunks
260g pack skinless and boneless cod fillet by Sainsbury's, cut into chunks
180g pack raw king prawns by Sainsbury's
Handful fresh flat-leaf parsley leaves, roughly chopped, to garnish
Finely grated parmesan, to serve

1   Heat the olive oil in a large heavy-based pot over a medium-high heat. Add the onion, garlic and celery and fry for 5-6 mins, until just beginning to soften.

2   Add the orange zest and juice, cayenne pepper, chopped tomatoes and fish stock to the pot, and gently stir to combine. Bring the soup to a simmer and continue to cook, uncovered, for 20 mins, until the celery is tender.

3   Reduce the heat to medium and add the salmon, cod and prawns. Cook for 2-3 mins, until the fish is cooked through, opaque and flakes easily, and the prawns are pink and cooked through.

4   Serve the soup garnished with the parsley and parmesan.

Per serving: 1439kJ/344kcal (17%), 17.7g fat (25%), 5.3g saturates (27%), 7.1g sugars (8%), 1.56g salt (26%)

Cook's tip
It's important not to overcook the fish in this recipe or it will be tough and rubbery. It will continue to cook in the bowl so serve it when the fish is just opaque and the prawns have only just turned pink.

Baby leaf spinach soup with salmon

Tender salmon and spinach are the heroes in this simple dish

2 tbsp olive oil
1 large onion, finely chopped
4 cloves garlic, sliced
1 potato, peeled and cut into 2cm cubes
1 tsp ground nutmeg
850ml vegetable stock, made
with 1 stock cube

500g frozen baby whole leaf spinach
by Sainsbury's
150ml semi-skimmed milk
135g pack Scottish honey roasted salmon
flakes by Sainsbury's
4 tbsp crème fraîche, to serve

1   Heat the oil in a large heavy-based pan and fry the onion and garlic over a
    medium heat for 4-5 mins until softened but not coloured. Add the potato and
    nutmeg, and continue to cook for a further 1 min.

2   Stir through the stock and simmer for 12-15 mins until the potato is tender. Add
    the spinach and milk, and bring the soup to a simmer, stirring constantly.

3   Let the soup cool off the heat a little, then use a hand blender to blend until
    smooth. Stir through half of the salmon flakes, ladle into bowls and serve
    garnished with the crème fraîche, black pepper and the remaining salmon flakes.
    Try serving with the Melba toasts (see below), if you like.

Per serving (without Melba toasts): 1279kJ/306kcal (15%), 17.3g fat (25%), 6.1g
saturates (31%), 6.1g sugars (7%), 1.31g salt (22%)

Melba toasts Ⓥ

Cut the crusts from 8 slices of white bread. Preheat
the grill to high and toast both sides of the bread.
Using a sharp, serrated bread knife and with a steady
hand, slice the bread horizontally. Cut the halved
bread into triangles and put back under the grill until
just golden and the edges have begun to curl.

Makes 16 Prep time: 5 mins Cook time: 5 mins
Per serving (4 toasts): 617kJ/146kcal (7%), 1.2g fat (2%),
0.3g saturates (2%), 2.6g sugars (3%), 0.47g salt (8%)

SERVES 4
PREP TIME 15 mins
COOK TIME 35 mins

Spiced parsnip soup with chestnuts

Warming spices, roasted root veg and sweet chestnuts come together for a welcome meal to come home to on a wet winter's night

750g parsnips, peeled and chopped into 3-4cm cubes
2 tbsp olive oil
2 onions, chopped
1 tsp each ground coriander, ground cumin, ground turmeric and ground ginger

1 litre vegetable stock, made with 1 stock cube
500ml semi-skimmed milk

FOR THE GARNISH
1 tbsp olive oil
100g cooked and peeled chestnuts, chopped

1   Preheat the oven to 200°C, fan 180°C, gas 6. Put the parsnips in a roasting tin and drizzle with 1 tbsp of the oil. Roast for 20 mins, turning once.

2   Meanwhile, heat the remaining oil in a large pan over a medium heat. Add the onions and fry for 2-3 mins before stirring in the spices. Continue to fry for a few mins more, until the onion has softened completely and is translucent.

3   Add the roasted parsnips and stock to the pan. Bring to the boil, cover and simmer for 10 mins. Allow to cool, then transfer to a blender and purée until smooth. Return to the pan and stir in the milk. Heat through gently.

4   Meanwhile, make the garnish. Heat the oil in a frying pan and gently fry the chopped chestnuts for 1-2 mins. Serve the roasted parsnip soup in mugs or bowls, topped with the hot chestnuts and some freshly ground black pepper.

Per serving: 1509kJ/360kcal (18%), 13.1g fat (19%), 3.2g saturates (16%), 23.5g sugars (26%), 1.25g salt (21%)

Cook's tip
To prepare fresh chestnuts, soak them in cold water for 30 mins, then score with a knife on the plump side. Roast on a baking tray at 200°C, fan 180°C, gas 6 for about 25 mins, then peel away the hard outer shell and the softer inner brown skin while the nuts are still warm.

SERVES 4
PREP TIME 25 mins
COOK TIME 35 mins

Borscht

This vibrant beetroot soup is a winter staple in Eastern Europe

1 tbsp vegetable oil

1 onion, finely chopped

225g raw beetroot, peeled and grated

1 small carrot, peeled and diced

1 stick celery, trimmed and diced

1 tsp allspice

500g potatoes, peeled and diced

1.2 litres vegetable stock, made with

1 stock cube

¼ red cabbage, shredded

2 tbsp red wine vinegar

4 tbsp soured cream

Snipped fresh chives, to garnish

1   Heat the vegetable oil in a heavy-based pan over a medium heat, then add the onion. Soften for 4-5 mins before adding the beetroot, carrot, celery and allspice. Mix well, cover and cook for a further 6-8 mins, stirring occasionally to stop the vegetables catching on the bottom of the pan.

2   Stir in the potatoes, stock and red cabbage, then simmer for about 20 mins, until the vegetables are tender.

3   Stir in the red wine vinegar, then let cool slightly. Blend with a hand blender, until you have a silky texture, season to taste, then return to the pan to heat through.

4   Divide between 4 bowls and serve topped with the soured cream and a scattering of chives.

Per serving: 1072kJ/255kcal (13%), 7.2g fat (10%), 2.5g saturates (13%), 13g sugars (14%), 1.31g salt (22%)

Cook's tip
To avoid staining your hands, wear rubber gloves to peel and grate the beetroot.

bakes & pies

Roast chicken with winter root vegetables	30
Chicken, ham & mustard pot pies	32
Chicken & pesto gnocchi bake	34
Bacon hotpot	36
Purple sprouting broccoli with herb butter	36
Bacon lattice pie	38
Roasted garlic mash	38
Cumberland pie	40
Steak & mushroom Guinness pie	42
Lamb pastitsio	44
Irish stew pie	46
Fiery Spanish cod bake	48
Trout & courgette gratin	50
Bean enchiladas	52
Aubergine parmigiana	54
Veggie filo bake	56
Game pie	58
Venison & turnip pie	60

SERVES 4
PREP TIME 25 mins
COOK TIME
2 hours 15 mins

Roast chicken with winter root vegetables

An easy way to roast a chicken, with the veg and gravy all in one tin

300g carrots, peeled and cut into chunks
2 medium parsnips, peeled and cut
into chunks
2 medium turnips, peeled and cut into
thin wedges
2 red onions, peeled and thickly sliced
6 cloves garlic, unpeeled
1 lemon, cut into wedges

3 fresh bay leaves
2 tbsp olive oil
1.35kg British whole chicken by Sainsbury's
1 tbsp Dijon mustard
600ml chicken stock, made with 1 stock cube
1 tbsp wholegrain mustard
3 tbsp clear honey
2 tsp cornflour

1   Preheat the oven to 190ºC, fan 170ºC, gas 5. Cook the carrots, parsnips and turnips in a pan of boiling water for 8-10 mins. Drain, then transfer to a large flameproof roasting tin. Add the onions, garlic, lemon and bay leaves to the tin. Drizzle over 1 tbsp of the oil and toss the vegetables to coat. Sit the chicken on top of the vegetables. Mix the remaining oil with the Dijon mustard and spoon half over the chicken, spreading it all over the skin with your fingers. Pour half the stock into the tin.

2   Roast for 1 hour, until the chicken skin is golden. Cover loosely with foil and roast for a further 30 mins, or until the chicken is cooked through: the juices should run clear when a skewer is inserted into the thickest part of the thigh.

3   Transfer the chicken to a large warmed platter, cover and set aside. Increase the oven temperature to 220ºC, fan 200ºC, gas 7. Mix the wholegrain mustard and honey with the remaining Dijon mustard and oil mixture, and gently stir into the vegetables in the roasting tin. Return the tin to the oven and roast for a further 25-30 mins, until the vegetables are tender and golden at the edges.

4   Transfer all the veg to the platter. Pour the rest of the stock into the roasting tin and scrape with a spoon to loosen any bits. Pour into a small pan, then bring to the boil over a medium heat. Blend the cornflour to a paste with a little cold water and stir into the hot liquid. Simmer for 3-4 mins, stirring, until the gravy thickens. Serve the chicken and vegetables with the mustard gravy.

Per serving: 2435kJ/581cal (29%), 23.2g fat (33%), 5.6g saturates (28%), 28.7g sugars (32%), 1.83g salt (31%)

Chicken, ham & mustard pot pies

Using ready-cooked meat and a prepared sauce makes these tasty pies simple to prepare and quick to bake

480g pack 4 ready-cooked roast chicken
breast fillets by Sainsbury's
200g piece cooked smoked ham, from
the instore deli counter
350g tub fresh Italian three-cheese
sauce by Sainsbury's
100ml semi-skimmed milk

1 tbsp wholegrain mustard
Small handful fresh flat-leaf parsley,
leaves picked and chopped
4 tbsp frozen garden peas
375g pack ready-rolled puff pastry
by Sainsbury's
1 medium egg, beaten

1 Preheat the oven to 200°C, fan 180°C, gas 6. Remove the skin from the chicken breasts and cut the chicken and ham into small chunks. Empty the sauce into a mixing bowl and whisk in the milk. Add the chicken, ham, mustard, parsley and peas, stir to combine and season with freshly ground black pepper.

2 Unroll the puff pastry and, using the rim of one of 4 x 275ml pie or other ovenproof dishes as a guide, cut out 4 circles of pastry slightly bigger than the dishes. Divide the filling between the dishes, then brush the rims with some of the beaten egg.

3 Cover each dish with a circle of pastry, pressing down gently to seal. Brush the pastry lids with the remaining egg. Put on a baking tray and bake for 15-20 mins, or until the pastry is puffed and golden.

Per pie: 2204kJ/527cal (26%), 25.7g fat (37%), 13g saturates (65%), 4.1g sugars (5%), 3.01g salt (50%)

Cook's tip
Re-roll the pastry trimmings, cut out shapes and use to decorate the pies, sticking them on with beaten egg.

SERVES 4
PREP TIME 10 mins
COOK TIME 25 mins

Chicken & pesto gnocchi bake

A satisfying, all-in-one bake that's not too heavy – serve it with salad leaves if you like, or some steamed green beans on the side

1 tbsp olive oil
4 spring onions, trimmed and finely sliced
300ml half-fat crème fraîche
4 tbsp red pesto
240g pack cooked roast chicken fillets by Sainsbury's, skin removed and discarded, and meat shredded

500g pack fresh Italian gnocchi by Sainsbury's
100g baby spinach
150g cherry tomatoes on the vine, cut in half, plus 1 stem with the tomatoes attached
20g grated parmesan
Fresh basil leaves, to garnish

1   Preheat the oven to 200°C, fan 180°C, gas 6. Heat 2 tsp of the oil in a large deep frying pan. Add the spring onions and fry gently for 2-3 mins. Stir in the crème fraîche and pesto, and simmer for 2-3 mins, until you have a creamy sauce.

2   Meanwhile, bring a large pan of water to the boil. Add the gnocchi and boil for 1-2 mins, until the gnocchi rise to the surface. Drain well and stir into the creamy pesto sauce with the chicken, spinach and the halved cherry tomatoes. Remove the pan from the heat and season to taste with freshly ground black pepper.

3   Transfer the gnocchi mixture to a large shallow ovenproof dish, scatter over the parmesan and top with the stem of tomatoes. Drizzle over the rest of the oil and bake in the oven for 18-20 mins, until golden and bubbling. Serve garnished the basil.

Per serving: 2222kJ/531cal (27%), 25.7g fat (37%), 10.5g saturates (53%), 5.4g sugars (6%), 2.06g salt (34%)

SERVES 4
PREP TIME 20 mins
COOK TIME
1 hour 20 mins –
1 hour 25 mins

Bacon hotpot

This warming hotpot is layered with leek, apples, potatoes and bacon

---

15g unsalted butter, softened
800g Maris Piper potatoes, peeled
and very thinly sliced
1 large leek, trimmed and sliced
1 large red apple, halved, cored and
thinly sliced

250ml dry cider
1 tsp Dijon mustard
4 rashers thick-cut unsmoked back
bacon by Sainsbury's, roughly chopped
Few fresh sage leaves

---

1   Preheat the oven to 190°C, fan 180°C, gas 5. Use some of the butter to grease
    a shallow 2-litre ovenproof baking dish.

2   Layer the sliced potatoes, leek and apple in the dish, seasoning every couple of
    layers with a little freshly ground black pepper. In a jug, mix the cider with the
    mustard and pour into the dish.

3   Dot the potatoes, leek and apples with the remaining butter and scatter the
    bacon pieces and sage leaves on top. Cover with foil and bake in the preheated
    oven for 1 hour, until the potatoes are almost tender. Remove the foil and bake
    for a further 20-25 mins, until the bacon is crisp and the top layer of potatoes is
    just golden. Serve with the purple sprouting broccoli and herb butter (see below),
    if you like.

Per serving (without broccoli and herb butter): 1499kJ/356cal (18%), 11.4g fat
(16%), 4.8g saturates (24%), 8.7g sugars (10%), 0.09g salt (2%)

Purple sprouting broccoli with herb butter

Beat 50g softened butter with 1 tbsp each chopped
fresh thyme and parsley, 1 tsp lemon zest and some
freshly ground black pepper. Steam 300g purple
sprouting broccoli and 1 thinly sliced red onion for
8-10 mins. Transfer to a dish and toss with the butter.

Serves 4 Prep time: 5 mins Cook time: 8-10 mins
Per serving: 592kJ/143kcal (7%), 11.3g fat (16%), 6.3g saturates
(32%), 3.8g sugars (4%), <0.01g salt (<1%)

Bacon lattice pie

A lattice-style finish not only looks impressive but uses less pastry, too

1 tbsp olive oil
1 onion, finely chopped
1 clove garlic, crushed
2 carrots, peeled and sliced on the diagonal
625g smoked bacon loin, fat trimmed and discarded, and bacon cut into cubes
20g pack parsley sauce mix by Sainsbury's

300ml semi-skimmed milk
250g broccoli, cut into small florets
200g frozen garden peas
½ x 375g pack ready rolled lighter puff pastry by Sainsbury's
1 medium egg, beaten

1 Preheat the oven to 180°C, fan 160°C, gas 4. Heat the oil in a large pan, add the onion and cook for 5 mins, until softened. Add the garlic, carrots and bacon and cook for a further 5 mins.

2 Meanwhile, make up the parsley sauce to pack instructions using the milk. Stir it into the bacon mixture, and add the broccoli and peas. Season to taste and transfer the mixture to a 1.5 litre pie dish.

3 Unroll the puff pastry and cut into 2cm-wide strips. Arrange the strips over the top of the pie filling, trimming any excess pastry, and then brush all over with the beaten egg. Bake in the oven for 25-30 mins, until the pastry is golden and the filling is bubbling. Serve with roasted garlic mash (see below), if you like.

Per serving: 2259kJ/540cal (27%), 26.5g fat (38%), 9.8g saturates (49%), 13.7g sugars (15%), 4.34 salt (72%)

Roasted garlic mash Ⓥ

Preheat the oven to 200°C, fan 180°C, gas 6. Break 1 bulb garlic into cloves. Put the cloves, unpeeled, in a foil parcel, drizzle with 2 tsp olive oil, seal and roast for 12-15 mins. Peel 1kg potatoes and cut into chunks. Put in a pan, cover with cold water and bring to the boil. Cook for 15-20 mins. Drain. Mash with 4 tbsp milk and 25g butter. Remove the garlic from the oven and squeeze out the flesh into the mash. Season to taste.

Serves 4 Prep time: 10 mins Cook time: 15-20 mins
Per serving: 1088kJ/259kcal (13%), 7.4g fat (11%),
3.5g saturates (18%), 2.4g sugars (3%), 0.64g salt (11%)

SERVES 6
PREP TIME 25 mins
COOK TIME 1 hour
50 mins

Cumberland pie

The crispy breadcrumb and leek topping makes this pie extra special

1 tbsp sunflower oil

2 leeks, trimmed and thinly sliced

1 large onion, chopped

275g carrots, peeled and diced

500g pack 5% fat beef mince by Sainsbury's

100ml red wine

350ml beef stock, made with ½ stock cube

2 tbsp sun-dried tomato paste

2 tbsp Worcestershire sauce

1½ tsp dried mixed herbs

175g frozen garden peas

1kg Maris Piper potatoes, peeled and cut into chunks

2 tbsp semi-skimmed milk

40g unsalted butter

20g fresh white breadcrumbs

1   Heat the oil in a large deep frying pan and fry the leeks over a medium heat for 2-3 mins, until softened. Remove with a slotted spoon and set aside. Add the onion and carrots to the pan and fry for 5 mins, until softened, then add the mince and fry for 10 mins, stirring all the time, until cooked through with no pink colour remaining.

2   Stir in the wine and bubble for 1-2 mins, then add the stock, tomato paste, Worcestershire sauce and mixed herbs. Bring to the boil, reduce the heat, cover and simmer for 35 mins, stirring occasionally. Stir in the frozen peas and two-thirds of the fried leeks, then simmer, uncovered, for a further 10 mins. Season to taste.

3   Meanwhile, put the potatoes in a large pan of cold water. Bring to the boil and cook for 15-20 mins, until tender. Drain well, return to the pan and mash with the milk and half the butter, until smooth. Season to taste. Preheat the oven to 200°C, fan 180°C, gas 6.

4   Transfer the mince mixture to a 2-litre ovenproof dish and spoon the mashed potato on top. Melt the remaining butter and brush over the mash. Scatter over the remaining fried leeks and the breadcrumbs and bake in the oven for 35-40 mins. Cover the pie with foil 15 mins before the end of cooking time to prevent the leeks from burning.

Per serving: 1851kJ/442cal (22%), 20.1g fat (29%), 8.8g saturates (44%), 9.5g sugars (11%), 1.01g salt (17%)

SERVES 6
PREP TIME 20 mins
COOK TIME
2 hours 20 mins –
3 hours 45 mins

Steak & mushroom Guinness pie

A classic flavour combination that makes a satisfying winter dinner

2 tbsp sunflower oil

600g lean diced casserole steak, from the instore meat counter

400g shallots, peeled and halved

2 tbsp plain flour

400ml Guinness

2 tbsp Worcestershire sauce

250ml beef stock, made from 1 stock cube

2 fresh bay leaves

250g closed-cup chestnut mushrooms, quartered

375g pack ready-rolled puff pastry by Sainsbury's

1 medium egg, beaten

200g Tenderstem broccoli, steamed, to serve

200g mangetout, steamed, to serve

1   Heat half the oil in a deep flameproof casserole. Add the steak in batches and cook over a high heat until browned all over, adding a little more of the remaining oil, if necessary. Remove with a slotted spoon and set aside.

2   Add the rest of the oil and the shallots to the casserole, and fry over a medium heat for 5 mins. Sprinkle over the flour and cook for 1-2 mins, then gradually pour in the Guinness, Worcestershire sauce and stock and bring to the boil.

3   Return the steak to the casserole, add the bay leaves and mushrooms and season to taste. Reduce the heat to a simmer, cover with a tight-fitting lid and cook for 1 hour 30 mins to 2 hours, until the steak is very tender.

4   Preheat the oven to 220°C, fan 200°C, gas 7. Use a slotted spoon to transfer the steak and vegetables to a 2-litre pie dish and discard the bay leaves. Bubble the liquid in the casserole for 8-10 mins, until it's reduced by one-third. Pour the gravy over the meat and vegetables. Brush the rim of the pie dish with egg.

5   Unroll the pastry and drape over the pie dish. Trim off any excess pastry and press to seal the edges. Score criss-cross lines lightly across the top of the pastry with the tip of a knife and pierce 2-3 holes in the pastry to let the steam escape. Brush all over with the remaining egg.

6   Bake for 25-30 mins, until the pastry is risen and golden. Serve with the vegetables.

Per serving: 2048kJ/488cal (24%), 20g fat (29%), 8.3g saturates (42%), 6.7g sugars (7%), 1.49g salt (25%)

SERVES 6
PREP TIME 15 mins
COOK TIME 1 hour 10
mins – 1 hour 20 mins

Lamb pastitsio

Layers of lamb ragù, pasta and béchamel sauce make this traditional Greek bake a hearty choice for a chilly evening

1 tbsp olive oil

1 red onion, finely chopped

2 cloves garlic, crushed

500g pack 20% fat minced lamb by Sainsbury's

390g carton Italian chopped tomatoes by Sainsbury's

2 tsp dried oregano

¼ tsp ground cinnamon

½ tsp sugar

1 tbsp sun-dried tomato purée

450ml semi-skimmed milk

40g butter

40g plain flour

300g penne pasta

1 egg, beaten

50g mature Cheddar, grated

1 Heat the oil in a large deep frying pan and fry the onion and garlic over a medium heat for 5-6 mins, until softened. Add the lamb, turn the heat up to high and fry for 5-6 mins, stirring, until cooked through with no pink colour remaining.

2 Stir in the tomatoes, oregano, cinnamon, sugar, tomato purée and 200ml water. Bring to the boil, then reduce the heat and simmer, uncovered, for 25 mins, stirring occasionally. Season to taste.

3 Meanwhile, make the sauce. Put the milk, butter and flour in a large pan and slowly bring to the boil, whisking, until smooth and thickened. Season to taste, then stir in half the cheese and simmer for a further 2-3 mins. Preheat the oven to 180°C, fan 160°C, gas 4.

4 Cook the pasta in a large pan of boiling water for 8-10 mins until just al dente. Drain well. Spread half the pasta over the base of a 2-litre ovenproof dish (at least 6cm deep) and spoon over about one-third of the cheese sauce. Top with the mince mixture, then the remaining pasta.

5 Beat the egg into the rest of the cheese sauce and spoon over the pasta. Scatter over the rest of the cheese. Bake for 35-40 mins until the top is golden and bubbling. Serve with a green salad, if you like.

Per serving: 2554kJ/610kcal (31%), 30.5g fat (44%), 15g saturates (75%), 9.8g sugars (11%), 0.58g salt (10%)

SERVES 6
PREP TIME
35 mins, plus
chilling and cooling
COOK TIME
2 hours 40 mins

Irish stew pie

Full of wintry flavours, this traditional stew in pie form will be a winner

1 tbsp sunflower oil
700g joint boneless half shoulder of lamb, trimmed of excess fat and cut into chunks
1 large onion, thickly sliced
200g carrots, peeled and cut into chunks
250g swede, peeled and cut into chunks
1 tbsp flour
450ml lamb stock, made with 1 stock cube
1 fresh bay leaf

Few sprigs fresh thyme
125g Savoy cabbage, roughly chopped

FOR THE PASTRY
200g plain flour, plus extra for dusting
1 tsp dried mixed herbs
100g chilled unsalted butter, diced
1 egg, beaten

1   Preheat the oven to 160°C, fan 140°C, gas 3. Heat the oil in a flameproof casserole and fry the lamb in batches over a high heat for 4-5 mins until browned. Remove with a slotted spoon and set aside.

2   Add the onion, carrots and swede to the casserole, and cook over a medium heat for 5 mins. Stir in the flour and cook for 30 seconds, then gradually pour in the stock and bring to the boil. Stir in the bay leaf and thyme and season lightly. Cover and cook in the oven for 1 hour 30 mins to 2 hours, until the meat and vegetables are very tender.

3   Meanwhile, make the pastry. Put the flour, mixed herbs and butter in a food processor with some freshly ground black pepper. Whiz to fine breadcrumbs, then add 2-3 tbsp ice-cold water and process to a crumbly dough. Turn out and knead lightly until smooth. Wrap in cling film and chill until the stew is cooked.

4   When the stew is cooked, stir in the cabbage, then transfer to a 1.5-litre pie dish and leave to cool for 20 mins. Remove the pastry from the fridge and increase the oven temperature to 190°C, fan 170°C, gas 5.

5   Roll out the pastry on a lightly floured surface to a circle or oval just larger than the top of the pie dish. Brush the rim of the dish with a little of the beaten egg and drape the pastry over the dish. Press the edges down to seal and trim off the excess pastry. Pierce 2-3 holes in the top of the pastry and glaze with the rest of the egg. Bake for 40-45 mins, until the pastry is crisp and golden.

Per serving: 2205kJ/528kcal (26%), 28.3g fat (40%), 13.9g saturates (70%), 7.7g sugars (9%), 0.48g salt (8%)

Fiery Spanish cod bake

Chorizo and smoked paprika give this delicious fish dish an unmistakably Spanish flavour - it's perfect with warm crusty bread

1 tbsp olive oil
½ x 225g Spanish chorizo ring
by Sainsbury's, sliced
1 onion, cut into thin wedges
2 red chillies, deseeded and thinly sliced
1 large red pepper, deseeded and sliced
4 large vine tomatoes, halved, then each
half quartered

500g skinless and boneless cod loin, from
the instore fish counter, cut into chunks
140g tub manzanilla and Kalamata
olives by Sainsbury's, drained
1-2 tsp smoked paprika
Chopped fresh flat-leaf parsley, to garnish
½ x 400g crusty white baguette,
warmed, to serve

1   Preheat the oven to 200°C, fan 180°C, gas 6. Heat half the oil in a large
    nonstick frying pan and fry the chorizo over a medium heat for 1 min, until
    it starts releasing oil. Remove with a slotted spoon and set aside.

2   Add the onion and chillies to the pan and fry for 4-5 mins, stirring, until they
    start to soften. Stir in the pepper and tomatoes, and cook for a further 3-4 mins.
    Transfer to a 2-litre shallow ovenproof dish. Nestle the cod chunks among the
    vegetables, then scatter over the chorizo and olives.

3   Season with plenty of freshly ground black pepper, sprinkle over the smoked
    paprika, then drizzle over the remaining oil. Bake in the oven for 25-30 mins,
    until the cod is cooked through - it should be opaque and flake easily.

4   Serve garnished with the parsley, with the warm crusty baguette to mop up the
    spicy juices.

Per serving: 2154kJ/514kcal (26%), 22g fat (31%), 6.2g saturates (31%),
9.7g sugars (11%), 2.79g salt (47%)

Cook's tip
You can use other fish for this tasty bake - for an
extra-smoky flavour, try smoked cod or haddock.
A few cooked, peeled fresh prawns can be added, too.

SERVES 4
PREP TIME 20 mins
COOK TIME 20 mins

Trout & courgette gratin

With a slightly more delicate flavour, trout makes a great alternative to salmon. The capers add a sharp, savoury edge to this gratin

2-3 slices ciabatta

2 tbsp olive oil

1 onion, cut into thin wedges

2 x 220g packs fresh Scottish loch trout fillets by Sainsbury's

400g courgettes, trimmed and cut into thick chunks

4 tbsp half-fat crème fraîche

2 tbsp semi-skimmed milk

2 tsp baby capers, drained and rinsed

1 clove garlic, crushed

50g Gruyère cheese, finely grated

1   Preheat the grill to medium-high then toast the ciabatta until crisp and golden on both sides. Cool for a few mins, then break into pieces and tip into a food processor. Process briefly to make coarse crumbs, then set aside.

2   Heat 1 tbsp of the oil in a frying pan and fry the onion wedges over a high heat for 2-3 mins, until just golden, then remove from the heat.

3   Meanwhile, bring a large shallow pan of water to the boil. Reduce the heat, add the trout fillets and simmer gently for 2-3 mins, until just cooked. Remove with a slotted spoon and set aside to cool for a few mins. Bring the water back to the boil, add the courgettes and cook for 1-2 mins, until almost tender. Drain well and transfer to a 2-litre shallow ovenproof dish.

4   Break the trout into chunks, discarding any skin and bones, and nestle among the courgettes. Scatter the fried onions over the top and season to taste. Preheat the oven to 220°C, fan 200°C, gas 7.

5   Mix together the crème fraîche and milk until smooth, then spoon over the trout, courgettes and onions. Toss the ciabatta crumbs with the remaining oil, the capers, garlic and cheese, then scatter over the trout mixture. Bake in the preheated oven for 10-15 mins, until the crumb topping is crisp and golden.

Per serving: 1799kJ/432kcal (22%), 27.9g fat (40%), 9.7g saturates (49%), 5.5g sugars (6%), 0.57g salt (10%)

SERVES 4
PREP TIME 15 mins
COOK TIME
35-40 mins

Bean enchiladas

Bring some spicy Mexican flavours to the dinner table with this mouthwatering meat-free meal idea

1 tbsp sunflower oil, plus extra for greasing
7 spring onions, trimmed and finely sliced
1 clove garlic, crushed
1 red pepper, deseeded and finely chopped
1 red chilli, deseeded and finely chopped
420g tin mixed beans in mild chilli sauce
by Sainsbury's

230g tin Italian chopped tomatoes
by Sainsbury's
Pinch of sugar
4 soft flour tortillas
75g mature Cheddar, grated
150ml soured cream

1   Preheat the oven to 200°C, fan 180°C, gas 6. Lightly grease a 2-litre shallow ovenproof dish.

2   Heat the 1 tbsp oil in a large frying pan. Add the chopped spring onions (reserve a handful to garnish), garlic, red pepper and half of the chopped chilli, and fry over a medium heat for 3-4 mins, until softened, stirring occasionally.

3   Stir in the beans in chilli sauce, chopped tomatoes and sugar. Bring to the boil, reduce the heat and simmer for 5-6 mins, stirring occasionally, until the sauce has thickened a little. Season to taste.

4   Divide the bean mixture between the tortillas, top with some of the Cheddar and roll up, tucking in the ends. Place side-by-side in a single layer in the baking dish (they should fit together snugly). Spoon over the soured cream and scatter over the remaining cheese and chopped chilli.

5   Cover with foil and bake in the oven for 10 mins, then uncover and bake for a further 15-20 mins until the cheese is golden and bubbling. Serve garnished with the reserved spring onion.

Per serving: 1750kJ/418kcal (21%), 19.3g fat (28%), 10g saturates (50%), 11.7g sugars (13%), 1.53g salt (26%)

SERVES 4
PREP TIME 15 mins
COOK TIME
50-55 mins

Aubergine parmigiana

Try this Italian-inspired bake - aubergines never tasted so good!

2½ tbsp olive oil

1 onion, finely chopped

2 cloves garlic, crushed

2 tsp dried oregano

500g passata

2 tsp balsamic vinegar

1 tsp sugar

Small handful fresh basil leaves, roughly torn, plus extra leaves to garnish

2 aubergines, thinly sliced

35g grated parmesan

200g mozzarella, torn into small pieces

270g Taste the Difference ciabatta loaf, baked, to serve

1   Heat 1 tbsp of the oil in a large pan over a medium heat. Add the onion, garlic and dried oregano, and fry gently for 5-6 mins, stirring occasionally, until the onions are softened and just starting to brown.

2   Stir in the passata and 100ml water, and bring to the boil. Reduce the heat, cover and simmer gently for 15 mins, stirring occasionally, until thickened. Stir in the vinegar, sugar and torn basil leaves, then cook for a further 1 min. Season to taste.

3   Meanwhile, put the aubergine slices in a large shallow dish and drizzle over the rest of the oil, tossing to lightly coat. Heat a large cast iron griddle pan over a medium heat and cook the aubergine slices, in batches, for 1-2 mins on each side until brown and just tender. If you don't have a griddle pan, grill the slices instead. Preheat the oven to 190°C, fan 170°C, gas 5.

4   Spoon a thin layer of the tomato sauce over the base of a 1.5-litre shallow ovenproof dish. Top with a sprinkling of parmesan, then a single layer of aubergine slices. Repeat until all the ingredients are used up (reserving 2 tsp parmesan for the top), finishing with a layer of tomato sauce.

5   Top with the torn mozzarella and reserved parmesan, then season with freshly ground black pepper. Put the dish on a baking sheet and bake in the preheated oven for 30-35 mins until the top is golden and bubbling. Serve garnished with the extra basil leaves, with warm ciabatta bread.

Per serving: 2049kJ/489kcal (25%), 22.5g fat (32%), 9.8g saturates (49%), 15.1g sugars (17%), 1.66g salt (28%)

SERVES 8
PREP TIME 30 mins
COOK TIME 1 hour
20 mins

Veggie filo bake

This nutty dish is inspired by baklava and makes an impressive
meat-free meal, especially for entertaining

2 tbsp olive oil

750g leeks, trimmed and sliced

1½ tbsp chopped fresh thyme

200g walnut halves

2 large cloves garlic, sliced

2 x 390g cartons chopped tomatoes
by Sainsbury's

1½ tbsp sherry vinegar

350g young leaf spinach

125g unsalted butter, melted

12 sheets filo pastry

200g goats' or sheep's cheese
(or a mixture of the two)

5 tbsp clear honey

400g each of steamed and shredded kale
and runner beans, to serve

1   In a large frying pan, heat 1 tbsp of the oil and fry the leeks over a high heat
    for 8 mins, stirring regularly, until soft, then stir in the thyme. Meanwhile, in
    another frying pan set over a medium heat, toast the walnut halves for 10 mins,
    until browned, shaking the pan from time to time, then roughly chop.

2   In a third pan, heat the remaining oil and fry the garlic for 1-2 mins, until fragrant.
    Add the tomatoes and vinegar and simmer for 20-30 mins, until thick and
    reduced. Add the spinach and stir over the heat for 3-5 mins, until the spinach
    has wilted and any water released has evaporated. Season to taste.

3   Preheat the oven to 180°C, fan 160°C, gas 4. Brush the inside of a 35cm x 20cm
    roasting tray with melted butter. Lay 4 sheets of filo on the base, brushing
    each sheet with melted butter before adding the next. Spread half the leeks
    over the pastry, top with half the walnuts and crumble or grate over half the
    cheese. Drizzle with a third of the honey, then spoon over half the tomato and
    spinach mixture.

4   Repeat with another 4 sheets of filo, buttering between each sheet, then the
    fillings, and finishing with the final sheets of filo pastry. Stir the remaining honey
    into the leftover butter and brush all over the top, drenching the pastry. Score
    the top in a diamond pattern and bake for 40-45 mins, until golden brown and
    piping hot. Serve with steamed runner beans and kale.

Per serving: 2535kJ/610kcal (31%), 42g fat (60%), 14.4g saturates (72%),
18.7g sugars (21%), 0.52g salt (9%)

Game pie

A rich pie using our seasonal casserole mix – a combination of venison, pheasant, pigeon, partridge, duck and rabbit in varying quantities, depending on the season. Lamb makes a tasty alternative, if preferred

1 tbsp olive oil
½ x 250g pack smoked bacon lardons by Sainsbury's
2 x 340g packs Taste The Difference game casserole mix by Sainsbury's
2 red onions, thickly sliced
2 cloves garlic, crushed
4 carrots, peeled and diced
1 swede, peeled and diced
1½ tbsp flour

300ml beef stock, made with ½ stock cube
300ml full-bodied red wine
1 fresh bay leaf
Few sprigs fresh thyme
Zest of 1 orange
1-2 tbsp redcurrant jelly
1 medium egg, beaten, to glaze
375g pack ready rolled lighter puff pastry by Sainsbury's
Mashed potato, to serve

1 Heat the oil in a large flameproof casserole dish over a medium heat. Add the bacon and fry for 5-6 mins. Remove with a slotted spoon and set aside. Add the game meat mix to the casserole dish and brown all over – you'll need to do this in batches. Remove with a slotted spoon and set aside with the bacon.

2 Add the onions to the casserole dish and fry over a medium heat for 5 mins, adding 1 tbsp of water if they begin to stick. Stir in the garlic, carrots and swede and cook for 2-3 mins, then add the flour and cook, stirring, for 1 min. Pour in the stock and wine, and bring to the boil.

3 Return the bacon and game mixture to the casserole dish and add the herbs and orange zest. Season to taste with freshly ground black pepper and reduce the heat to a gentle simmer. Cover and simmer for 1 hour 15 mins or until the meat is tender, skimming the surface every so often. Remove the herbs and discard. Season. Stir in the redcurrant jelly and simmer for a few mins until melted. Transfer the casserole mixture to a 1.5-litre pie dish and brush the rim of the dish with some of the egg. Preheat the oven to 220°C, fan 200°C, gas 7.

4 Unroll the pastry and drape over the pie dish. Trim off any excess pastry and press the edges to seal. Decorate with pastry trimmings, then brush with the rest of the egg. Pierce 2-3 holes in the top; bake for 30 mins. Serve with the mash.

Per serving: 2857kJ/680kcal (34%), 23.5g fat (34%), 8.8g saturates (44%), 14.7g sugars (16%), 2.38g salt (40%)

SERVES 4
PREP TIME 20 mins
COOK TIME 2 hours

Venison & turnip pie

A seasonal pie with a deep, rich flavour – if you can't find venison, use beef casserole steak instead

2 x 340g packs Taste the Difference diced wild venison

2 tbsp plain flour

2 tbsp sunflower oil

200g shallots, peeled and halved

2 cloves garlic, finely chopped

4 celery sticks, trimmed and chopped

350g turnips, peeled and cut into chunks

15g unsalted butter

200ml beef stock, made with ½ stock cube

300ml brown ale

Few juniper berries, roughly crushed

2 sprigs fresh rosemary

1 medium egg, beaten

375g pack ready-rolled shortcrust pastry by Sainsbury's

1   Preheat the oven to 170°C, fan 150°C, gas 3. Pat the venison dry with kitchen paper. Put the flour and a little salt and freshly ground black pepper in a plastic food bag. Add the venison, seal, and shake to coat.

2   Heat half the oil in a large flameproof casserole over a medium heat, add the shallots and fry for 5 mins, then stir in the garlic, celery and turnips and fry, stirring frequently, for 10 mins. Remove with a slotted spoon and set aside.

3   Add the rest of the oil and the butter to the pan and fry the meat, in batches, over a high heat until browned. Remove and set aside. Add any flour left in the bag to the casserole, along with the stock and ale, scraping any residue from the base of the casserole. Bring to the boil, then add the juniper berries and rosemary. Return the vegetables and venison to the casserole. Cover and cook in the oven for 1 hour, until the meat is tender.

4   Use a slotted spoon to transfer the meat and vegetables to a 1.5-litre pie dish. Put the casserole with the remaining liquid over a medium heat and simmer for about 10 mins until reduced by half. Pour over the meat and vegetables. Increase the oven temperature to 190°C, fan 170°C, gas 5 and brush the edges of the pie dish some of the egg.

5   Unroll the pastry and drape over the pie dish. Trim off any excess pastry and press to seal the edges. Decorate with pastry trimmings, then brush all over with the egg. Pierce 2-3 holes in the top and bake for 25 mins until golden.

Per serving: 2941kJ/704kcal (35%), 38.2g fat (55%), 16.5g saturates (83%), 9.1g sugars (10%), 1.09g salt (18%)

on the hob

Chicken & squash barley risotto

Using barley instead of rice gives this risotto an unusual twist

---

1 tbsp extra-virgin olive oil flavoured with chilli
1 onion, chopped
400g butternut squash, peeled, deseeded
and cut into chunks
1 clove garlic, chopped
400g pack diced British chicken
breast by Sainsbury's

300g pearl barley
1 litre hot chicken stock, made
with 1 stock cube
80g young leaf spinach
Small handful fresh flat-leaf parsley,
leaves picked and chopped
4 tbsp freshly grated parmesan

---

1 Heat the chilli oil in a large shallow pan. Add the onion and cook over a medium heat for 5 mins, to soften.

2 Add the butternut squash and garlic, cook for 2 mins, then add the diced chicken. Cook for 5 mins, stirring occasionally, until the chicken is no longer pink.

3 Stir in the pearl barley and cook for 1 min, then pour in a quarter of the hot chicken stock. Bring to the boil, then reduce the heat and simmer, stirring frequently, until the stock is absorbed.

4 Add another quarter of the stock and simmer, stirring, until absorbed. Repeat with the remaining stock, adding it one-quarter at a time, until the barley is tender but still nutty. This will take about 40 mins, during which time the butternut squash will soften.

5 Season with freshly ground black pepper and stir in the spinach until the leaves are just wilted. Stir in the parsley and half of the parmesan. Serve sprinkled with the remaining parmesan and some extra freshly ground black pepper.

Per serving: 1635kJ/389kcal (20%), 11.4g fat (16%), 4.1g saturates (21%), 6.9g sugars (8%), 1.41g salt (24%)

Cook's tip
If you prefer the squash to be firm, add it half way through the cooking time.

Pan-fried duck with herb & orange stuffing

Great for a special occasion, this simple dish has the wow factor

---

4 skin-on duck breast fillets
50g fresh white breadcrumbs
Small handful fresh flat-leaf parsley, finely chopped
Few sprigs fresh thyme, chopped
Finely grated zest and juice of 1 orange

1 egg, beaten
200ml chicken stock, made with ½ stock cube
2 tbsp fine-cut orange marmalade
2 tsp cornflour
350g fine green beans, steamed, to serve

---

1 Slice the duck breasts in half horizontally, keeping them attached at one side, and open out like a book.

2 Mix together the breadcrumbs, herbs, orange zest and egg; season with freshly ground black pepper. Spoon over the duck and enclose by folding back the top half of each breast. Secure by tying each breast at intervals with kitchen string.

3 Heat a large non-stick frying pan until hot. Prick the skin on the duck breasts several times with a fork or sharp knife and place in the hot pan, skin-side down. Cook over a high heat for 5 mins until crisp and golden, then turn, reduce the heat slightly, cover and cook for a further 10 mins.

4 Remove the duck breasts from the pan and set aside to rest. Pour off the excess fat from the pan (keep this for frying potatoes in, if you like), then add the chicken stock, marmalade and nearly all of the orange juice (reserve 1 tbsp to mix with the cornflour in step 5). Bring the mixture to the boil, stirring, then reduce the heat and simmer for 3 mins.

5 Mix the cornflour with the reserved orange juice until smooth and add to the sauce, stirring until thickened slightly. Return the duck breasts to the pan, cover and simmer in the sauce for 10 mins until cooked through.

6 Remove the duck breasts from the pan and allow to rest for 5 mins. Remove the string, then slice and serve with the steamed green beans and orange sauce.

Per serving: 2027kJ/483kcal (24%), 19.8g fat (28%), 5.3g saturates (27%), 10.1g sugars (11%), 1.23g salt (21%)

Chicken chasseur with vegetable mash

A hearty chicken stew that will fill your kitchen with mouthwatering aromas while it bubbles away on the hob

1 tbsp sunflower oil
4 whole chicken legs
1 onion, chopped
½ x 160g twin-pack Taste the Difference oak smoked ultimate outdoor bred bacon lardons
200g baby button mushrooms
2 cloves garlic, crushed
100ml dry white wine
1 tbsp tomato purée

1 tbsp Worcestershire sauce
300ml chicken stock, made with 1 stock cube
3 sprigs fresh thyme, plus extra sprigs to garnish

FOR THE VEGETABLE MASH
1 small swede, peeled and diced
400g carrots, peeled and diced

1 Heat the oil in a large deep frying pan. Season the chicken legs with freshly ground black pepper and fry for 10 mins, turning once, until browned all over.

2 Add the onion, bacon and mushrooms; fry over a medium heat for a further 5 mins. Add the garlic and wine, bring to the boil, then reduce the heat and simmer for 3 mins.

3 Stir the tomato purée and Worcestershire sauce into the chicken stock, then pour into the pan. Add the thyme sprigs, bring to the boil, then reduce the heat, cover and simmer for 40 mins, until the chicken is cooked through.

4 Meanwhile, make the mash. Put the vegetables in a pan of cold water. Bring to the boil and simmer for 20-25 mins until tender. Drain, return to the pan and mash. Serve with the chasseur garnished with the extra thyme sprigs.

Per serving: 2394kJ/574kcal (29%), 33.2g fat (47%), 9.9g saturates (50%), 18.3g sugars (20%), 2.52g salt (42%)

Cook's tip
Chicken leg portions are the thigh with the drumstick attached. They're great value and ideal for braising, as the meat stays succulent and falls off the bone.

Turkey forestière

Tender turkey in an earthy, creamy mushroom and wine sauce

½ x 30g pack dried portobello mushrooms by Sainsbury's
2 tbsp sunflower oil
4 turkey breast steaks
1 onion, sliced

2 cloves garlic, chopped
250g chestnut mushrooms, sliced
100ml Marsala wine
150ml fresh double cream
Small handful fresh flat-leaf parsley, chopped

1 Tip the dried mushrooms into a heatproof bowl and pour over 100ml boiling water from the kettle. Leave to soak for 10 mins.

2 Meanwhile, heat 1 tbsp of the oil in a large frying pan. Season the turkey with freshly ground black pepper and fry over a medium heat for 10 mins, turning once, until browned. Transfer to a plate and set aside.

3 Add the onion to the pan with the remaining oil, cook for 5 mins, then add the garlic and chestnut mushrooms. Drain the soaked dried mushrooms, reserving the soaking liquid, and add to the pan. Cook for 5 mins, stirring occasionally.

4 Pour in the wine and the mushroom soaking liquid, bring to the boil, then reduce the heat and simmer for 5 mins to reduce slightly. Pour in the cream and bring to the boil, stirring. Return the turkey to the pan, add the parsley and season with freshly ground black pepper. Cover and simmer for 10 mins. Serve with the kale (see below), if you like.

Per serving (without kale): 1807kJ/433kcal (22%), 25.3g fat (36%), 12.4g saturates (62%), 5.5g sugars (6%), 0.29g salt (5%)

Sautéed kale with hazelnuts Ⓥ

Melt 25g unsalted butter in a large frying pan. Add 2 x 200g packs curly leaf kale and toss until coated all over with the melted butter. Cover with a lid and cook for 5 mins until the kale is just tender. Add the juice of ½ lemon and 25g roasted chopped hazelnuts. Stir well, season with freshly ground black pepper and serve with the turkey forestière.

Serves 4 Prep time: 5 mins Cook time: 8 mins
Per serving: 511kJ/124kcal (6%), 10.4g fat (15%), 3.6g saturates (18%), 1.4g sugars (2%), <1g salt (<1%)

Liver & bacon with creamy mash

A simple, traditional meal that's packed with delicious flavour

360g pack lambs' liver by Sainsbury's

1 tbsp sunflower oil

2 onions, sliced

8 rashers smoked streaky bacon

3 tbsp plain flour

2 tsp English mustard powder

450ml tub beef stock by Sainsbury's

1 tbsp Worcestershire sauce

400g steamed cabbage, to serve (optional)

FOR THE CREAMY MASH

1kg Maris Piper potatoes, cut into chunks

25g unsalted butter

4 tbsp single fresh cream

1 Remove and discard any membranes from the liver, then set aside. Heat the oil in a medium pan, add the onions and cook over a low heat for 15 mins, until soft.

2 Meanwhile, start the mash. Put the potatoes in a pan of cold water, bring to the boil, then reduce the heat and simmer, covered, for 20-25 mins until very tender.

3 Dry-fry the bacon in a large non-stick frying pan over a medium-high heat for 5 mins, turning occasionally, until browned and cooked through. Set aside.

4 Put the flour, mustard powder and some freshly ground black pepper in a plastic food bag, then shake to mix. Remove 1 tbsp of the mix and stir into the onions; cook for 1 min, then add the beef stock. Bring to the boil, stirring, then reduce the heat, add the Worcestershire sauce and simmer gently while you cook the liver.

5 Add the liver to the bag of seasoned flour and shake to coat. Remove the bacon from the frying pan, put on a plate and cover to keep warm. Fry the liver in the hot bacon fat over a medium heat for 10 mins, turning once, until browned. Sprinkle in any remaining flour from the bag, stir into the pan juices then pour over the onion gravy. Simmer for 2-3 mins until the liver is cooked through.

6 Meanwhile, drain the potatoes and return to the pan. Add the butter and mash. Add the cream and mash again. Serve the liver with the onion gravy spooned over the mash, with the bacon and steamed cabbage, if using.

Per serving: 3166kJ/754kcal (34%), 26.9g fat (38%), 11.2g saturates (56%), 10.4g sugars (12%), 2.62g salt (44%)

Classic beef casserole

Tender, melt-in-the-mouth beef, a thick, rich gravy and plump, herb dumplings make this one-pot classic the ultimate winter warmer

2 tbsp plain flour
691g twin-pack diced casserole
steak by Sainsbury's
2 tbsp sunflower oil
12 shallots, peeled
2 carrots, peeled and cut into chunks
300ml dark ale
1 tbsp tomato purée

300ml beef stock, made with ½ stock cube
3 sprigs fresh thyme
1 fresh bay leaf
142g pack dumpling mix by Sainsbury's
2 tsp creamed horseradish
Small handful fresh flat-leaf parsley,
roughly chopped

1   Tip the flour into a plastic food bag and season with freshly ground black pepper. Add the beef, seal and shake to coat.

2   Heat half the oil in a flameproof casserole. Over a high heat, fry half the beef for 5 mins, turning occasionally, until browned all over. Remove with a slotted spoon, put on a plate and set aside. Repeat with the remaining oil and beef.

3   Add the shallots and carrots to the casserole, cook over a medium heat for 3 mins, until starting to soften, then add any remaining flour from the bag. Cook for a further 1 minute.

4   Return the beef to the casserole with any juices from the plate and pour in the ale. Stir the tomato purée into the beef stock, then add to the casserole with the thyme sprigs and bay leaf. Bring to the boil, then reduce the heat, cover and simmer for 1 hr 40 mins, stirring occasionally, until the meat is tender.

5   Just before the end of the cooking time, make up the dumpling mix according to pack instructions, stirring the horseradish and parsley into the water before adding to the dumpling mix. Shape into 8 small balls. Uncover the casserole and gently place the dumplings on top. Cover and cook for a further 20 mins, unstil the dumplings are light and fluffy.

Per serving: 1614kJ/384kcal (19%), 12.5g fat (18%), 4g saturates (20%), 11.1g sugars (12%), 1.51g salt (25%)

Rib-eye steak with Stilton & hollandaise

Juicy steaks made memorable with a punchy, blue cheese sauce

4 rib-eye steaks, seasoned with freshly
ground black pepper and rubbed with a
little olive oil
70g baby leaf watercress
20g Stilton, crumbled
Sautéed garlic potatoes, to serve
(see recipe below)

FOR THE STILTON HOLLANDAISE
2 tbsp white wine vinegar
½ shallot, peeled and finely chopped
A few black peppercorns, lightly crushed
45g lighter buttersoft by Sainsbury's
1 tbsp semi-skimmed milk
1 medium egg yolk

1 Make the hollandaise. Heat the vinegar with the shallot, peppercorns and 2 tbsp water in a pan. Bring to the boil and simmer until reduced by half. Strain into a jug, discarding the shallots and peppercorns. Melt the buttersoft in the same pan. Blend the yolk in a mini food processor. With the motor running, pour in the vinegar reduction and milk, then gradually pour in the melted buttersoft until you have a thick sauce. Season to taste.

2 Heat a griddle pan until hot. Add the steaks and sear for 2-3 mins. Turn and cook for 3 mins for medium or 4-5 mins for well-done. Rest for 5 mins, then serve with the sauce, crumbled Stilton, watercress and potatoes.

Per serving (1 steak with sauce and vegetables): 3338kJ/799kcal (40%), 45.6g fat (65%), 19.3g saturates (97%), 7.8g sugars (9%), 0.71g salt (12%)

Sautéed garlic potatoes Ⓥ

Peel and chop 500g each of sweet potatoes and Maris Piper potatoes. Put in a pan of cold water, bring to the boil and cook for 5 mins. Drain. Heat 4 tbsp olive oil in a frying pan, add the potatoes and 3 unpeeled cloves garlic. Cook over a medium heat, turning occasionally, for 10 mins, until golden. Squeeze the garlic from their skins, mash and stir into the potatoes. Season to taste.

Serves 4 Prep time: 15 mins Cook time: 20 mins
Per serving: 1279kJ/305kcal (15%), 10.6g fat (15%), 1.6g saturates (8%), 7.9g sugars (9%), 0.13g salt (2%)

Pork & winter vegetable stir-fry

A delicious dish that makes the most of seasonal vegetables

2 tbsp groundnut oil
400g pack British pork leg escalopes by Sainsbury's, cut into thin strips
2 tsp runny honey
200g celeriac, peeled and cut into thin batons
200g butternut squash, peeled, deseeded and cut into thin batons
1 leek, trimmed, cut into 6cm lengths, then cut into thin batons
200g red cabbage, shredded
1 clove garlic, crushed
3cm piece fresh root ginger, peeled and finely grated
Juice of 1 lime
2 tbsp sweet chilli dipping sauce

1   Heat the oil in a large wok or frying pan until hot. Add the pork and stir-fry over a high heat for 2 mins. Add the honey and stir-fry for a further 1 min until the pork is browned all over. Transfer to a plate with a slotted spoon.

2   Add the celeriac and butternut squash to the wok or frying pan and stir-fry for 5 mins until starting to soften (reduce the heat and add a splash of water if the vegetables start to stick).

3   Add the leek and red cabbage, stir-fry for 2 mins, then return the pork to the wok or frying pan. In a small bowl, mix the garlic with the ginger, lime juice and sweet chilli sauce. Add to the pan and cook for 3 mins until the pork is hot and cooked through with no pink colour remaining and the vegetables are just tender but still have a slight crunch.

Per serving: 1192kJ/284kcal (14%), 10.1g fat (14%), 1.9g saturates (10%), 12.7g sugars (14%), 0.67g salt (11%)

Cook's tip
This is a great recipe for using up any extra vegetables you may have in the fridge. Shredded raw Brussels sprouts or Savoy cabbage make a good addition to, or replacement for, the red cabbage.

SERVES 4
PREP TIME
10 mins, plus 15 mins
standing and resting
COOK TIME
5-10 mins

Ras el hanout lamb with tabbouleh

Our version of the popular Middle Eastern salad is given a Moroccan twist with the addition of coriander and pomegranate seeds

2 tsp ras el hanout spice mix by Sainsbury's
1 clove garlic, crushed
1 tbsp olive oil
1 tsp clear honey
4 lamb rump steaks

FOR THE TABBOULEH
125g bulgar wheat
500ml hot vegetable stock, made with 1 stock cube
1 small red onion, finely chopped
Few sprigs each fresh flat-leaf parsley, coriander and mint, roughly chopped
50g pomegranate seeds
Grated zest and juice of ½ lemon

1 Mix together the ras el hanout, garlic, oil and honey to make a paste. Put the lamb steaks on a plate and spread the spice paste over both sides of the meat. Cover loosely and leave to stand while you make the tabbouleh.

2 Put the bulgar wheat in a heatproof bowl and pour over the hot stock. Cover with cling film and leave to stand for 15 mins, until all the stock has been absorbed and the grains have swollen. Fluff up the grains with a fork and stir in the onion, chopped herbs, pomegranate seeds, and lemon zest and juice. Season to taste.

3 Heat a griddle pan or large frying pan until hot. Sear the lamb for 2-3 mins each side for medium or 4-5 mins each side for well-done. Leave to rest for 5 mins, then serve with the tabbouleh.

Per serving: 1533kJ/367kcal (18%), 18.8g fat (27%), 7g saturates (35%), 6g sugars (7%), 1.38g salt (23%)

Cook's tip
For a more traditional tabbouleh, add finely chopped tomato instead of pomegranate seeds, omit the coriander and use 1 part mint to 4 parts parsley.

One-pot lamb with olives & spinach

This all-in-one dish is packed with warming Mediterranean flavours. Serve it on creamy polenta instead of with crusty bread, if you like

1 tbsp olive oil

767g boneless lamb shoulder joint by Sainsbury's, cut into chunks

1 onion, thickly sliced

2 cloves garlic, finely sliced

1 large red pepper, deseeded and cut into chunks

A few fresh rosemary sprigs

500ml chicken stock, made with 1 stock cube

Small handful fresh flat-leaf parsley, chopped

150ml half-fat crème fraîche

410g tin haricot beans, drained and rinsed

335g cherry tomatoes

90g pitted black olives

100g baby leaf spinach

Crusty bread, to serve

1   Heat the oil in a large flameproof casserole over a high heat. Add the lamb in batches and cook until browned all over. Remove with a slotted spoon and set aside on a plate.

2   Add the onion, garlic and pepper to the casserole and fry for 5-6 mins, then return the lamb and any meat juices from the plate to the casserole. Stir in the rosemary and stock, reduce the heat, cover and simmer gently for 1 hour, until the lamb is tender.

3   Meanwhile, mix the parsley and crème fraîche together in a small bowl. Season with freshly ground black pepper.

4   Stir the beans, tomatoes and olives into the casserole and simmer, uncovered, for 30 mins, until the liquid has reduced and the tomatoes are very soft. Stir in the spinach and season to taste with freshly ground black pepper.

5   Serve in warm shallow bowls with the parsley and crème fraîche sauce, with crusty bread on the side.

Per serving: 3742kJ/892kcal (45%), 37.8g fat (54%), 16g saturates (80%), 10.3g sugars (11%), 2.85g salt (48%)

Pollock, black olive & preserved lemon tagine

Pollock is a great, sustainable alternative to cod, but you could use any firm white fish you like in this fragrant Moroccan dish

2 tbsp olive oil
1 red onion, chopped
2 garlic cloves, finely chopped
1 tsp each ground cumin, ginger and cinnamon
½ x 180g jar preserved sliced lemons by Sainsbury's, drained and chopped
150ml dry white wine

200ml fish stock, made with ½ stock cube
Large pinch of saffron strands
1 tsp clear honey
12 cherry tomatoes, halved
50g dry black olives
600g pollock fillets, cut into chunks
Chopped fresh coriander leaves, to garnish

1 Heat the oil in a large pan, add the onion and cook over a medium heat for 5 mins until soft. Add the garlic, spices and lemons and cook for 2 mins.

2 Pour in the wine and fish stock, add the saffron and honey and bring to the boil. Add the tomatoes and olives, reduce the heat and simmer for 5 mins.

3 Add the pollock, cover and simmer gently for 10 mins until the fish is opaque and flakes easily. Sprinkle with the coriander and serve with harissa couscous (see below), if you like.

Per serving (without harissa couscous): 1134kJ/271kcal (14%), 12.8g fat (18%), 2g saturates (10%), 5.6g sugars (6%), 1.82g salt (30%)

Harissa couscous

Pour 350ml hot vegetable stock into a heatproof bowl, then stir in 2 tsp harissa paste and 250g couscous. Cover with cling film and leave for 5 mins, until all the stock has been absorbed. Fluff up the grains, then add a handful of chopped fresh mint and 1 tbsp oil from a jar of preserved sliced lemons by Sainsbury's. Season to taste.

Serves 4 Prep time: 5 mins, plus standing
Per serving: 1131kJ/267kcal (13%), 4.1g fat (6%), 0.9g saturates (5%), <0.5g sugars (<1%), 1.07g salt (18%)

Pan-fried trout with vegetable & lentil ragù

Rustic, braised lentils are the perfect cold-weather accompaniment to crisp-skinned trout fillets

2 tbsp olive oil
1 onion, chopped
1 medium carrot, peeled and chopped
2 sticks celery, trimmed and chopped
1 clove garlic, crushed
200g lentilles vertes by Sainsbury's
400ml vegetable stock, made with
1 stock cube

Few sprigs of fresh thyme
1 fresh bay leaf
4 x 150g boneless trout fillets, from the instore fish counter
150g fine green beans, cut into 3cm lengths
Small handful fresh flat-leaf parsley, leaves picked and chopped
Lemon wedges, to serve

1   Heat half the oil in a large pan, add the onion, carrot and celery and cook for 5 mins, stirring occasionally.

2   Add the garlic, lentils, stock, thyme and bay leaf. Bring to the boil, then reduce the heat, cover and simmer for 35 mins, until the lentils are tender, adding a little hot water or extra stock if the mixture becomes too dry.

3   Heat the remaining oil in a frying pan. Add the trout fillets, skin-side down, and fry for 5 mins, turning once, until it's cooked through, opaque and flakes easily.

4   Meanwhile, blanch the green beans in a pan of simmering water for 3-5 mins, until tender. Drain, then stir through the lentils with most of the parsley. Season to taste and serve with the trout fillets, lemon wedges and the rest of the parsley, to garnish.

Per serving: 1602kJ/382kcal (19%), 15.1g fat (22%), 4.5g saturates (23%), 5.9g sugars (7%), 1.33g salt (22%)

Cook's tip
Fry some chopped pancetta with the onion in step 1 to give the ragù a smoky flavour.

SERVES 4
PREP TIME 15 mins
COOK TIME 12 mins

Spaghetti with mussels and cockles

This delicious dish of chilli spiked spaghetti tossed with plump cockles and mussels is ready in less than half an hour

1kg fresh mussels, from the instore fish counter

350g spaghetti

4 tbsp olive oil

2 shallots, peeled and chopped

1 red chilli, sliced (with seeds)

2 cloves garlic, chopped

100ml dry white wine

2 x 90g packs cooked shelled cockles, from the chiller cabinet

Small handful fresh flat-leaf parsley, roughly chopped

1   Before you start cooking, scrub the mussels well, removing any beards, and discard any that don't close when tapped firmly on the work surface.

2   Bring a large pan of water to the boil. Add the spaghetti and cook for 10 mins until just tender.

3   While the spaghetti is cooking, heat the olive oil in a large shallow pan with a lid. Add the shallots and chilli and cook, stirring, over a medium heat for 3 mins. Add the garlic, wine and mussels; cover and cook over a high heat for 3-4 mins, until all the mussels have opened, shaking the pan occasionally. Discard any mussels that remain closed.

4   Add the cockles and parsley to the pan and heat for 2 mins. Season to taste with freshly ground black pepper. Drain the spaghetti and toss into the sauce just before serving.

Per serving: 2086kJ/495kcal (25%), 12.7g fat (18%), 2.4g saturates (12%), 4.6g sugars (5%), 2.26g salt (38%)

Cook's tip
If you can't find live mussels, use a 200g pack of cooked shelled mussels by Sainsbury's from the chiller cabinet instead, and prepare to pack instructions.

Catalan bean stew

A substantial meat-free stew with tomatoes, green pepper and two types of beans, that will warm you up on those wintry weeknights

---

3 tbsp olive oil

3 onions, chopped

1 green pepper, deseeded and cut into chunks

500g potatoes, peeled and cut into chunks

2 cloves garlic, chopped

300ml vegetable stock, made with 1 stock cube

4 large vine tomatoes, chopped

½ tsp dried chilli flakes

2 tsp smoked paprika

1 tbsp tomato purée

410g tin red kidney beans in water, drained and rinsed

215g tin butter beans in water, drained and rinsed

50g fresh white breadcrumbs

4 tbsp garlic mayonnaise, to serve

---

1 Heat 2 tbsp of the oil in a large pan. Add the onions and green pepper, and fry over a medium heat for 5 mins, until softened.

2 Add the potatoes and cook for a further 5 mins. Stir in the garlic, stock, tomatoes, chilli flakes, paprika and tomato purée. Bring to the boil, then reduce the heat, cover, and simmer for 15 mins, stirring occasionally.

3 Stir in the kidney and butter beans, season to taste, and simmer for 10 mins.

4 While the stew is cooking, heat the remaining oil in a small frying pan. Add the breadcrumbs and fry, stirring continuously, until crisp and golden. Serve the stew sprinkled with the crispy breadcrumbs, with a spoonful of the garlic mayonnaise.

Per serving: 1990kJ/475kcal (24%), 20.6g fat (29%), 2.7g saturates (14%), 14g sugars (16%), 1.28g salt (21%)

Cook's tip

To make your own garlic mayonnaise, simply stir 1 crushed clove garlic into 150g regular mayonnaise.

Italian-style veg stew

This chunky vegetable stew is pure comfort food in a bowl. Serve with crusty buttered bread and shavings of parmesan

2 tbsp olive oil

1 onion, chopped

2 large carrots, peeled and sliced

3 sticks celery, trimmed and cut into chunks

390g carton chopped Italian tomatoes with basil and oregano by Sainsbury's

500ml pouch vegetable stock by Sainsbury's

1 courgette, trimmed, halved and sliced

100g casarecce pasta shapes

410g tin borlotti beans in water, drained and rinsed

198g tin sweetcorn in water, drained and rinsed

200g Savoy cabbage, shredded

4 tbsp green pesto by Sainsbury's

Fresh basil leaves and parmesan shavings, to serve

1   Heat the oil in a large deep pan. Add the onion, carrots and celery, and cook for 5 mins until softened.

2   Add the chopped tomatoes and stock to the pan. Bring to the boil, then reduce the heat, cover and simmer for 15 mins.

3   Add the courgette, pasta, beans, sweetcorn and cabbage. Stir well, bring back to the boil, then cover and simmer for 10 mins, until the vegetables and pasta are just tender.

4   Ladle the stew into bowls and stir a spoonful of green pesto into each bowl. Serve garnished with the basil leaves and parmesan shavings, and seasoned with freshly ground black pepper.

Per serving: 1578kJ/376kcal (19%), 13g fat (19%), 2.4g saturates (12%), 17.6g sugars (20%), 1.68g salt (28%)

Cook's tip

We've used courgette and carrot but you can use any vegetables that are in season, or even a few handfuls of frozen mixed vegetables.

Huevos rancheros

An easy version of the popular spicy Mexican breakfast dish that's perfect for sharing any time of the day

2 tbsp olive oil

2 onions, chopped

1 red and 1 green pepper, deseeded and chopped

2 cloves garlic, chopped

1 red chilli, deseeded and chopped

250g passata

4 large eggs

Fresh coriander leaves, to garnish

Hot chilli sauce, to serve

1   Heat the olive oil in a large frying pan with a lid. Add the onions and peppers, and cook over a low heat for 10 mins, until soft.

2   Add the garlic, chilli and passata. Stir well and simmer for 10 mins, until the sauce has reduced and thickened slightly.

3   Make four small wells in the mixture and gently crack an egg into each. Cover the pan and cook for 5 mins, until the egg whites have set but the yolks are still soft.

4   Garnish with the coriander leaves and serve from the pan with the hot chilli sauce on the side.

Per serving: 859kJ/206kcal (10%), 10.9g fat (16%), 2.6g saturates (13%), 11.8g sugars (13%), 0.76g salt (13%)

Cook's tip

To make this dish a more substantial meal, stir in some chopped tomatoes and a carton of drained and rinsed black beans with the passata, and serve with boiled rice on the side.

Highland venison casserole

This hearty casserole is also delicious made with beef instead of venison

3 tbsp olive oil

1 large onion, finely diced

3 sticks celery, trimmed and finely diced

250g baby Chantenay carrots, peeled and tops trimmed

4 large cloves garlic, crushed

25g dried wild mushrooms, soaked in 200ml boiling water

2 x 340g packs Taste the Difference diced wild venison

3 tbsp plain flour

25g unsalted butter

300ml beef stock, made with ½ stock cube

300ml full-bodied red wine

A few sprigs of fresh thyme

1 sprig of fresh rosemary

3 fresh bay leaves

1 tsp balsamic vinegar

250g chestnut mushrooms, halved

Steamed green beans, to serve

1 Heat 2 tbsp of the oil in large flameproof casserole and fry the onion over a low heat for 5 mins, until soft. Add the celery and cook for 5 mins. Add the carrots and garlic and continue to cook for 10 mins, until just turning golden. Stir in the wild mushrooms, reserving the liquid, and cook for 2 mins.

2 Pat the venison dry with kitchen paper. Put the flour and a little salt and freshly ground black pepper in a plastic food bag. Add the venison, seal and shake to coat.

3 Remove the vegetables from the casserole and set aside, then add the remaining oil and the butter to the casserole. Add the venison in batches and fry over a high heat, until browned. Remove each batch with a slotted spoon and set aside. When the last batch is browned, return all the venison to the casserole along with the vegetables. Stir in any flour left in the plastic bag.

4 Slowly add the stock, red wine and mushroom soaking liquid. Add the herbs and vinegar and bring to the boil. Cover and simmer over a low heat for 1 hour 30 mins, adding a little water if needed. Add the chestnut mushrooms, cover and cook for a further 30 mins, until the venison is very tender.

5 Remove and discard the thyme and rosemary stalks. Serve the casserole with the steamed green beans.

Per serving: 1813kJ/433kcal (22%), 17.1g fat (24%), 6g saturates (30%), 9.3g sugars (10%), 0.61g salt (10%)

Marsala veal with vegetable remoulade

A speedy dish that looks impressive – perfect for midweek meals

8 slices of prosciutto
310g pack Taste the Difference British Freedom Food British veal escalopes (see Cook's tip)
4 fresh sage leaves
1 tbsp olive oil
20g butter
250ml Marsala wine
1 tsp balsamic vinegar

FOR THE REMOULADE
2 tbsp mayonnaise
1 tbsp Dijon mustard
Juice of ½ a lemon
½ white cabbage, cored and shredded
½ celeriac, peeled and shredded
2 medium fresh beetroot, trimmed, peeled and finely grated
2 tbsp baby capers, drained and rinsed

1 Wrap two slices of prosciutto around each veal escalope. Make a small incision in the top of each and tuck in a sage leaf. Set aside.

2 Make the remoulade. Put the mayonnaise, Dijon mustard and lemon juice in a mixing bowl and whisk until smooth. Stir through the vegetables and capers, and season to taste. Set aside while you cook the veal.

3 Heat the oil and the butter in a large frying pan until the butter starts to foam. Add the veal, sage leaf down, and fry for 2-3 mins. Turn and cook for another 2-3 mins until cooked through with no pink remaining. Remove and keep warm.

4 Add the wine and balsamic vinegar to the frying pan, increase the heat and deglaze the pan, scraping any bits of prosciutto from the bottom of the pan for extra flavour. Reduce until syrupy and serve with the escalopes and remoulade.

Per serving: 1530kJ/366kcal (18%), 17.2g fat (25%), 5g saturates (25%), 14.4g sugars (16%), 1.94g salt (32%)

Cook's tip
If you don't want to use veal, this recipe works just as well with thin beef frying steaks.

slow cook

SERVES 4
PREP TIME
15 mins, plus resting
COOK TIME 1 hour,
30 mins

Chicken & vegetable pot roast

An all-in-one Sunday roast that's sure to become a new family favourite. Be inventive with the veg and use whatever is in season

---

1 tbsp vegetable oil

250g pack smoked bacon lardons by Sainsbury's

400g shallots, soaked in boiling water, peeled and halved

2 carrots, peeled and roughly chopped

2 parsnips, peeled and roughly chopped

4 cloves garlic, chopped

1 tbsp plain flour

150ml dry sherry

700ml chicken stock, made with 1 stock cube

6 sprigs fresh thyme

2 fresh bay leaves

800g baby potatoes, halved if large

15g unsalted butter, softened

1.35kg whole British chicken by Sainsbury's

---

1 Heat the oil in a large flameproof casserole over a medium heat and cook the lardons for 4-5 mins, until crisp. Remove with a slotted spoon and set aside. Add the shallots, carrots and parsnips to the casserole and cook for 5 mins, until just golden. Stir in the garlic and flour, and cook for a further 1 min, stirring.

2 Gradually pour in the sherry and stock. Bring to a gentle simmer, stirring. Add the thyme, bay leaves and baby potatoes; return the lardons to the casserole.

3 Preheat the oven to 200°C, fan 180°C, gas 6. Rub the butter over the chicken skin, season with freshly ground black pepper and put on top of the vegetables in the casserole. Roast, uncovered, for 25 mins, until the skin is crisp and golden. Reduce the oven temperature to 180°C, fan 160°C, gas 4, cover the casserole and cook for 45 mins, until the chicken juices run clear when the thickest part of the leg is pierced with a skewer.

4 Remove the casserole from the oven and transfer the chicken to a warmed platter. Cover with foil and rest for 10-15 mins before carving. Season the vegetables and sauce to taste, if needed. Serve the chicken sliced, with the vegetables and sauce.

Per serving: 3503kJ/837kcal (42%), 39.8g fat (57%), 13.2g saturates (66%), 12.3g sugars (14%), 4.40g salt (73%)

Chicken in red wine

A dish that makes the most of inexpensive chicken legs by braising them slowly in wine until meltingly tender

1 tbsp vegetable oil
½ x 206g twin-pack cubetti di pancetta by Sainsbury's
4 whole British chicken legs by Sainsbury's
1 onion, chopped
2 carrots, peeled and chopped
2 sticks celery, trimmed and chopped
3 cloves garlic, finely chopped
35g plain flour

600ml French red wine (see cook's tip)
500ml chicken stock, made with 1 stock cube
2 fresh bay leaves
4 fresh thyme sprigs
1kg baby potatoes
200g baby button mushrooms
250g shallots, soaked in boiling water, peeled and halved

1 Heat the oil in a large flameproof casserole over a medium heat and cook the pancetta for 3-4 mins, until golden. Remove with a slotted spoon and set aside. Add the chicken legs and cook, skin-side down, for 5-6 mins, until golden; turn and cook for another 3-4 mins. Set aside with the pancetta.

2 Preheat the oven to 180°C, fan 160°C, gas 4. Add the onion, carrots and celery to the casserole and cook over a low heat for 10-15 mins, until tender. Stir in the garlic and the flour and cook for 1-2 mins, then stir in the red wine and chicken stock. Add the bay leaves, thyme, potatoes and fried pancetta, and stir well. Top with the chicken legs, transfer to the oven and cook for 45 mins.

3 Remove the casserole from the oven and stir in the mushrooms and shallots, making sure the chicken legs stay on top. Return to the oven and cook for a further 30 mins, until all the vegetables are tender and the chicken is cooked through. Serve in large shallow bowls with the sauce ladled over the top.

Per serving: 3106kJ/742kcal (37%), 35.9g fat (51%), 10g saturates (50%), 12g sugars (13%), 2.44g salt (41%)

Cook's tip
It's worth splashing out and using a good-quality full-bodied French red wine, such as a classic Burgundy or Pinot Noir, for this dish.

Chicken Provençal

Anchovies add a deep savoury note to this Mediterranean meal

1 tbsp olive oil

8 skin-on chicken thighs

1 onion, thickly sliced

2 small fennel bulbs, trimmed and sliced, fronds reserved

4 cloves garlic, chopped

8 anchovy fillets, finely chopped

6 sprigs fresh thyme, leaves picked and chopped

3 sprigs fresh rosemary, leaves picked and chopped

150ml red wine

2 x 390g cartons Italian chopped tomatoes by Sainsbury's

140g mixed pitted green and black olives

1 tsp light brown soft sugar

Small handful fresh curly parsley leaves, roughly chopped

250g brown rice, boiled, to serve

1 Heat the oil in a shallow flameproof casserole over a medium heat and cook the chicken thighs, skin-side down, for 5 mins, until golden. Turn and cook for a further 5 mins, then remove from the casserole with a slotted spoon and set aside. You may need to do this in 2 batches.

2 Preheat the oven to 180°C, fan 160°C, gas 4. Add the onion and fennel to the casserole and cook for 5-6 mins. Add the garlic, anchovies, thyme and rosemary and fry for a further 2-3 mins. Pour in the red wine and bring to a simmer. Cook for 1-2 mins, then stir in the chopped tomatoes, olives and sugar. Season to taste with freshly ground black pepper.

3 Cover the dish tightly and cook for 1 hour 30 mins, removing the lid for the last 15 mins. Garnish with the parsley and reserved fennel fronds, and serve with boiled brown rice.

Per serving: 3834kJ/916kcal (46%), 43.5g fat (62%), 10.5g saturates (53%), 13.1g sugars (15%), 2.48g salt (41%)

Cook's tip
Try serving this rich casserole over pasta or with creamy mash or polenta.

SERVES 4
PREP TIME
15 mins, plus salting and chilling
COOK TIME 2 hours 40 mins

Confit of duck with spiced plum compote

A rich, hearty yet elegant dish packed with flavour and warming spices

1 tsp black peppercorns

5 sprigs fresh thyme, plus extra to garnish

½ tsp Chinese five spice

1 tbsp demerara sugar

4 tbsp sea salt

4 duck legs

2 x 295g jars duck fat by Sainsbury's

2 x 400g packs Parmentier potatoes by Sainsbury's and green salad, to serve

FOR THE PLUM COMPOTE

4 shallots, diced

1 tsp olive oil

1 tsp Chinese five spice

300g ripe plums, destoned and roughly chopped

1 tbsp demerara sugar

Zest and juice of 1 lime

2 sprigs fresh lemon thyme

1 Use a mini food processor or pestle and mortar to whiz or pound the peppercorns, thyme, five spice, demerara sugar and 2 tbsp of the sea salt to a fine powder, then stir in the remaining salt. Pat the duck dry with kitchen paper, then rub all over with the salt mixture. Transfer to a non-metallic dish, cover with cling film and chill in the fridge for at least 12 hours, or preferably 24 hours.

2 Preheat the oven to 160°C, fan 140°C, gas 3. Rub the salt off the duck legs with a damp, clean kitchen cloth, then put them in a small flame-proof casserole. Spoon over the duck fat. Bring to a simmer on the hob, then cover and cook in the oven for 2 hours, turning after 1 hour. Transfer the duck to a shallow dish, let cool slightly and pour over the fat from the casserole. Cool, cover and chill in the fridge until ready to serve.

3 For the compote, soften the shallots in the oil on a low heat. Add the five spice and fry for 1 min. Add the plums, sugar, lime juice and lemon thyme, season with black pepper, then cover and cook for 20 mins, until the plums are soft. Discard the thyme, remove from the heat and stir in the zest. Keep warm.

4 Meawhile, preheat the oven to 200°C, fan 180°C, gas 6. Cook the potatoes according to the pack instructions. Scrape the excess fat from the duck and roast on a baking sheet for 15 mins. For crisp skin, pop under a hot grill for a further 5 mins. Serve with the potatoes, spiced plum compote and salad.

Per serving: 4138kJ/992kcal (50%), 57.8g fat (83%), 17.1g saturates (86%), 22.9g sugars (25%), 2.94g salt (49%)

SERVES 4
PREP TIME 15 mins, plus marinating and resting
COOK TIME 3 hours

Slow-roast fennel & coriander pork belly

Succulent belly pork, slow roasted until gorgeously tender, pairs perfectly with apples, which cut through the richness of the meat

2 tsp fennel seeds

1 tsp coriander seeds

1 tsp cumin seeds

1 tbsp clear honey

1 tbsp tomato purée

1.5kg pork belly joint, skin scored

1 tbsp vegetable oil

200ml white wine

300ml chicken stock, made with 1 stock cube

2 eating apples, cored and cut into thick wedges

3 onions, cut into wedges

2 whole star anise

445g jar red cabbage in sweet vinegar by Sainsbury's, drained, to serve

1 With a pestle and mortar, grind the fennel, coriander and cumin seeds, then mix together with the honey and tomato purée. Rub the mixture all over the pork meat (not the skin). Cover loosely with foil and set aside to marinate for at least 1-2 hours, or overnight in the fridge, if possible.

2 Preheat the oven to 220°C, fan 200°C, gas 7. Put the pork in a large roasting tin, skin-side up, pour over the oil, rub into the scored skin and season to taste with freshly ground black pepper. Roast in the preheated oven for 30 mins, then reduce the temperature to 170°C, fan 150°C, gas 3. Pour the white wine and stock into the tin around the pork and roast for a further 1 hour.

3 Remove the roasting tin from the oven. Lift out the pork and set aside. Stir the apples, onions and star anise into the roasting tin and put the pork back on top. Cover tightly with foil and continue to cook for another 1 hour 30 mins, until the meat is tender and falling apart.

4 Remove the roasting tin from the oven and transfer the pork to a warmed platter. Cover with foil and leave to rest for 20 mins. Meanwhile, stir a little water into the apples and onions to make a sauce and remove the star anise. Cut the pork into thick slices and serve with the roasted apples and onions, and red cabbage.

Per serving: 2397kJ/575kcal (29%), 36g fat (51%), 11.7g saturates (59%), 17.8g sugars (20%), 1.46g salt (24%)

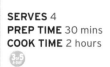
Sausage, pork & mixed bean stew

A satisfying stew that's packed with bold flavour

2 tbsp vegetable oil
250g pack smoked bacon lardons by Sainsbury's
250g diced pork shoulder
30g dried porcini mushrooms
1 onion, finely chopped
2 carrots, peeled and roughly chopped
2 sticks celery, trimmed and sliced
4 cloves garlic, finely chopped
150ml red wine
2 x 390g cartons Italian chopped tomatoes by Sainsbury's

1 tsp caster sugar
2 sprigs each fresh rosemary and sage, leaves picked and chopped
4 sprigs fresh thyme, leaves picked and chopped
340g pack British pork chipolatas by Sainsbury's
400g tin cannellini beans, drained and rinsed
400g tin butter beans, drained and rinsed
100g fresh white breadcrumbs
Small handful fresh flat-leaf parsley, leaves picked and chopped

1 Heat the oil in a large pan with an ovenproof handle and fry the lardons and diced pork for 5-10 mins, until golden. Remove from the pan and set aside.

2 Put the dried mushrooms in a bowl and cover with 250ml boiling water. Set aside for 10 mins to rehydrate. Drain, reserving the liquid. Chop the mushrooms; set aside.

3 Preheat the oven to 160ºC, fan 140ºC, gas 3. Fry the onion, carrots and celery for 10-15 mins in the pan you used to brown the meat, until softened, adding the garlic for the last 2 mins. Return the lardons and pork to the pan. Pour in the wine and simmer for 1 min. Stir in 300ml water, the tomatoes, porcini mushrooms and reserved liquid, sugar, rosemary, sage and thyme. Season to taste with freshly ground black pepper, then cover and cook in the oven for 1 hour.

4 Meanwhile, cook the sausages in a non-stick frying pan until golden. Stir into the stew with the beans, then continue to cook, covered, for a further 30 mins.

5 Turn the oven up to 200ºC, fan 180ºC, gas 6. Remove the pan from the oven. Mix the breadcrumbs with the parsley and season to taste. Scatter over the stew and return to the oven for 15 mins, until the top is golden.

Per serving: 3559kJ/851kcal (43%), 42g fat (60%), 12.9g saturates (65%), 17.7g sugars (20%), 3.91g salt (65%)

Sticky braised pork ribs with winter slaw

Meltingly tender plump pork ribs are what slow cooking is made for

2 x 500g pork rib racks
2 tbsp clear honey
½ tsp paprika
½ tsp hot chilli powder
1 tsp fennel seeds, ground
1 tsp ground cumin
¼ tsp garlic powder
1 tbsp Dijon mustard
250ml dry cider
150ml tomato ketchup
Zest and juice of ½ orange

3 tbsp balsamic vinegar
4 fresh thyme sprigs, leaves picked and chopped

FOR THE WINTER SLAW
2 carrots, peeled and coarsely grated
250g fresh beetroot, trimmed, scrubbed and cut into thin matchsticks
4 spring onions, trimmed and finely chopped
2 tbsp olive oil
2 tsp balsamic vinegar

1 Put the ribs in a large shallow dish. Mix together the honey, paprika, chilli powder, fennel, cumin, garlic powder and mustard in a small bowl. Brush all over the ribs. Cover and marinate in the fridge for 1-2 hours, or overnight if possible.

2 Preheat the oven to 150°C, fan 130°C, gas 2. Put the ribs in a large roasting tin. Heat the cider in a pan, then pour into the roasting tin around the ribs. Cover tightly with foil and cook in the oven for 1 hour.

3 Remove the ribs from the oven and pour the roasting tin liquid into a pan. Add the ketchup, orange juice and zest, vinegar and thyme to the pan. Bring to the boil and bubble for 5 mins, until thickened. Brush a quarter of the sauce over the ribs.

4 Increase the oven temperature to 180°C, fan 160°C, gas 4. Pour 200ml water into the roasting tin, but not over the ribs themselves. Return to the oven and cook, uncovered, for 1 hour, brushing with the sauce every 20 mins, until the ribs are very tender. If the roasting tin starts to look a little dry and the marinade starts to catch on the bottom, add a little more water.

5 Meanwhile make the winter slaw. Toss all the ingredients together in a bowl and season to taste with freshly ground black pepper. Serve with the hot sticky ribs.

Per serving: 1078kJ/258kcal (13%), 15.4g fat (22%), 4.9g saturates (25%), 14.3g sugars (16%), 0.45g salt (8%)

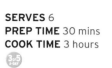

Braised beef, beetroot & port hotpot

Thanks to the addition of vibrant beetroot and rich port, this is a hotpot with a difference – serve it when you have guests over

---

2 tbsp plain flour

½ tsp ground allspice

650g braising beef, from the instore meat counter, diced

3 tbsp vegetable oil

400g shallots, peeled and halved

2 carrots, peeled and roughly chopped

500g fresh beetroot, trimmed, peeled and cut into thick wedges

200g chestnut mushrooms, thickly sliced

4 cloves garlic, finely chopped

8 sprigs thyme, leaves picked and chopped

150ml port

700ml beef stock, made with 1 stock cube

3 tbsp balsamic vinegar

75g blue cheese, roughly crumbled

500g celeriac, peeled and thinly sliced

600g Maris Piper potatoes, peeled and thinly sliced

15g unsalted butter, melted

---

1   Put the flour, allspice and a little salt and freshly ground black pepper in a plastic food bag. Add the beef, seal, and shake to coat. Heat 1 tbsp of the oil in a large flameproof casserole and fry half the beef over a high heat for 2-3 mins, turning, until browned. Remove with a slotted spoon and set aside. Heat another tbsp of the oil and brown the rest of the beef.

2   Preheat the oven to 160°C, fan 140°C, gas 3. Add the remaining oil to the casserole and cook the shallots and carrots over a medium heat for 10 mins, until golden. Add the beetroot and mushrooms and cook for 5-10 mins. Stir in the garlic, thyme, port, stock and balsamic vinegar. Bring to the boil, return the beef to the casserole, cover and cook in the oven for 1 hour 45 mins, until very tender.

3   Remove the casserole from the oven and increase the temperature to 180°C, fan 160°C, gas 4. Stir the blue cheese into the casserole and arrange the celeriac and potato slices on top in alternate layers, finishing with a layer of potatoes. Brush the top of the hotpot with the melted butter and return to the oven, uncovered, for 45 mins to 1 hour, until the potatoes are golden and tender.

Per serving: 2115kJ/504kcal (25%), 17.1g fat (24%), 6.3g saturates (32%), 18.0g sugars (20%), 1.58g salt (26%)

SERVES 4
PREP TIME 20 mins
COOK TIME
3 hours 15 mins

Asian-style brisket with noodles

Paired with fresh herbs, punchy chilli heat and crunchy pak choi, this slow-cooked beef with noodles makes an aromatic weekend supper

1 tbsp vegetable oil	1 tbsp fish sauce
1kg joint British beef brisket by Sainsbury's, string removed	100ml light soy sauce
3cm piece fresh ginger, peeled and finely chopped	40g light brown soft sugar
	125ml rice vinegar
4 cloves garlic, finely chopped	1 dried chilli (optional)
Large handful fresh coriander, stems and leaves chopped separately	Juice of 3 limes
2 lemongrass stalks, bashed and cut in half	150ml pineapple juice
2 red chillies, chopped	4 whole pak choi
	125g egg noodles
	4 spring onions, trimmed and sliced

1   Preheat the oven to 170°C, fan 150°C, gas 3. Heat the oil in a flameproof casserole. Cook the beef on all sides for 5 mins, until brown. Remove and set aside. Add the ginger, garlic, coriander stems, lemongrass and chillies, and cook for 2-3 mins, until fragrant. Stir in the fish sauce, soy sauce, sugar, rice vinegar, dried chilli (if using), and the lime and pineapple juices. Return the beef to the casserole and top up with 350ml water, so that it almost covers the beef. Cover and cook in the oven for 3 hours, until the meat is meltingly tender.

2   Remove the casserole from the oven, take the beef out and set aside to rest while you make the sauce. Put the dish over a medium heat and bring the liquid to a simmer. Bubble for 5 mins, until the sauce has reduced and thickened slightly. Remove and discard the lemongrass stalks and dried chilli.

3   Meanwhile, steam the pak choi for 3-4 mins and cook the noodles in boiling water for 2-3 mins. Drain.

4   Use two forks to shred the beef and serve with the sauce, pak choi and noodles, garnished with the spring onions and coriander leaves.

Per serving: 3635kJ/866kcal (43%), 33.9g fat (48%), 11.2g saturates (56%), 22.1g sugars (25%), 4.46g salt (74%)

SERVES 6, plus leftovers
PREP TIME 15-20 mins, plus resting
COOK TIME 4 hours 15 mins

Spicy shredded beef

A delicious way to roast beef that gives lots of lovely leftovers

2 tbsp vegetable oil

1.5kg joint British beef brisket, from the instore meat counter

6 shallots, peeled and finely chopped

4 cloves garlic, finely chopped

150ml red wine

250g passata

1 tsp light brown soft sugar

1 tbsp Dijon mustard

1 tsp hot paprika

1 tsp ground cumin

2 tsp dried oregano

1 tsp mild chilli powder

Zest and juice of ½ orange

1   Preheat the oven to 150°C, fan 130°C, gas 2. Heat the oil in a large flameproof casserole and fry the beef over a medium heat for 3-4 mins, turning occasionally, until browned all over. Remove and set aside.

2   Fry the shallots and garlic in the hot oil for 2-3 mins. Add the remaining ingredients and 150ml water. Bring to the boil and return the beef to the casserole.

3   Cover and cook in the oven for 4 hours, until the beef is completely tender. Turn the beef in the sauce every hour or so. Uncover for the last 30 mins.

4   Transfer the beef to a platter, cover with foil and rest for 10-15 mins, then use two forks to shred it. Strain the sauce through a sieve and stir into the beef to serve.

Per serving (125g brisket): 1542kJ/369kcal (19%), 19.2g fat (27%), 5.7g saturates (29%), 4.8g sugars (5%), 0.65g salt (11%)

Winter salad

Cook 150g bulgar wheat to pack instructions, adding 300g broccoli florets for the last 2-3 mins. Drain and rinse under cold water. Mix in a bowl with 2 grated carrots, ¹/₄ red cabbage, shredded, 100g spinach, shredded, 1 sliced red onion, 100g pomegranate seeds and 20g each pumpkin seeds and pine nuts. Dress with 6 tbsp French dressing and serve.

Serves 4 Prep time: 15 mins Cook time: 15 mins
Per serving: 1181kJ/282kcal (14%), 13.1g fat (19%), 1.2g saturates (6%), 15.2g sugars (17%), 0.34g salt (6%)

Beef cobbler

Rich, tender beef stew with a cheese and herb scone topping

2 tbsp plain flour
691g pack lean diced beef casserole steak by Sainsbury's
2 tbsp vegetable oil
½ x 250g pack smoked bacon lardons by Sainsbury's
400g shallots, peeled and halved
2 parsnips, peeled and thickly sliced
3 carrots, peeled and thickly sliced
2 leeks, trimmed and thickly sliced
3 cloves garlic, finely chopped
2 tbsp tomato purée

200ml ale
800ml beef stock, made with 1 stock cube
2 fresh bay leaves
4 sprigs fresh thyme
250g self-raising flour, sifted
50g unsalted butter, chilled and diced
100g mature Cheddar, finely grated
Few sprigs fresh flat-leaf parsley, chopped
125ml semi-skimmed milk, plus 1 tbsp for brushing
½ tsp Dijon mustard
2 tsp creamed horseradish

1   Tip the flour into a plastic food bag, add the beef and shake to coat. In a large flameproof casserole over a high heat, fry the beef in the oil for 2-3 mins until brown then remove and set aside. You may need to do this in batches.

2   Preheat the oven to 160°C, fan 140°C, gas 3. Add the lardons to the casserole and fry, stirring, for 4-5 mins. Add the shallots, parsnips, carrots and leeks, reduce the heat and cook gently for 10-15 mins, stirring occasionally.

3   Add the garlic and cook for 1 min, then stir in the tomato purée, ale, beef, stock, bay leaves and thyme, and bring to the boil. Season to taste with freshly ground black pepper, then cover and cook in the oven for 2 hours, until the beef and vegetables are very tender.

4   When the beef is cooked through, make the cobbler. In a bowl, rub together the flour, butter and a pinch of salt, until it resembles breadcrumbs. Stir in 75g of the Cheddar and the parsley. Whisk together the milk, mustard and horseradish, then stir into the flour mixture. Mix to a soft dough and shape into 8 scones.

5   Remove the casserole from the oven and increase the oven temperature to 200°C, fan 180°C, gas 6 and gently place the scones on the stew. Brush with the remaining milk and scatter over the remaining cheese. Return to the oven, uncovered, and cook for 10-15 mins, until the scones are risen and golden.

Per serving: 3685kJ/879kcal (44%), 35.8g fat (51%), 15.9g saturates (80%), 20.6g sugars (23%), 3.70g salt (62%)

Lamb shank, red wine & butterbean stew

Slow-cooked shanks are meltingly tender and a real crowd-pleaser. What's more, you can just add more shanks if you have more guests

1 tbsp olive oil

3 x packs 2 lamb shanks by Sainsbury's (each shank weighing 350-400g)

2 medium onions, sliced

2 sticks celery, trimmed and diced

2 carrots, peeled and diced

2 cloves garlic, crushed

2 tbsp plain flour

500ml fruity red wine, such as Shiraz

750ml vegetable stock, made with 1 stock cube

3 sprigs fresh rosemary

2 x 410g tins butter beans, drained and rinsed

1 Preheat the oven to 180°C, fan 160°C, gas 4. In a large flameproof casserole, heat the oil over a high heat. When hot, brown the lamb shanks all over – you'll need to do this in two batches. Remove and set aside, then add the onions and celery, cover, reduce the heat to low and cook, until soft and translucent.

2 Add the carrots, garlic and flour, increase the heat and cook, stirring, for 2 mins. Return the lamb shanks to the casserole, season to taste, then add the red wine, stock and rosemary. Bring to the boil, then cover and transfer to the oven for 1 hour 30 mins.

3 Remove the casserole from the oven and stir in the butter beans. Return to the oven and continue to cook, uncovered, for a further 30 mins. Transfer the lamb shanks to a plate, cover and keep warm. Strain the sauce (reserving the beans and vegetables and discarding the rosemary stalks) and return the liquid to the casserole. Boil on the hob for 15 mins, until reduced by a third. Stir the vegetables back into the sauce and pour over the lamb shanks to serve.

Per serving: 2661kJ/636kcal (32%), 31.2g fat (45%), 12.1g saturates (61%), 6.6g sugars (7%), 1.04g salt (17%)

Moroccan-style pot roast leg of lamb

Rubbed with a mix of North African spices and ingredients, this wonderfully tender leg of lamb will easily feed a crowd

1 tbsp ras el hanout

4 half slices preserved lemon by Sainsbury's, finely chopped

3 cloves garlic, finely chopped

1 tsp ground coriander

1 tsp ground cumin

2 tbsp vegetable oil

1.9kg leg of lamb, from the instore meat counter

200ml white wine

300ml chicken stock, made with 1 stock cube

410g tin chickpeas, drained and rinsed

1 tbsp harissa paste

50g dried apricots, chopped

2 bunches spring onions, trimmed and halved

2 x 270g packs Taste the Difference Vittoria tomatoes

250g couscous

1 tbsp toasted flaked almonds

Small handful fresh coriander, chopped

1 Mix together the ras el hanout, preserved lemon, garlic, coriander, cumin and vegetable oil in a small bowl. Pierce the lamb leg several times with the tip of a sharp knife, making sure the cuts are quite deep. Push some of the spice mix into the holes, then gently rub the rest over the joint. Cover and leave to marinate in the fridge for 1-2 hours, or overnight if possible.

2 Preheat the oven to 180°C, fan 160°C, gas 4. Put the lamb leg in a large roasting tin with the wine and stock, cover with foil and roast in the oven for 1 hour 30 mins. Remove the roasting tin from the oven, lift out the lamb joint and set aside. Stir the chickpeas, harissa paste and apricots into the hot liquid in the roasting tin. Add the spring onions and put the lamb joint back on top. Put the tomatoes around the lamb and roast, uncovered, for a further 30 mins.

3 Just before the end of the cooking time, put the couscous in a heatproof bowl and pour over 300ml boiling water. Cover and leave for 10 mins until all the liquid has been absorbed. Fluff up the grains with a fork, stir in the almonds and coriander, and season with freshly ground black pepper to taste. Carve the lamb and serve with the sauce and vegetables from the roasting tin.

Per serving (150g lamb): 2696kJ/642kcal (32%), 22.3g fat (32%), 6.1g saturates (31%), 8.6g sugars (10%), 1.43g salt (24%)

Lamb & aubergine bake

A Greek-style dish you can serve straight from oven to table

---

2 tbsp light olive oil
600g lamb neck fillets, cut into large pieces
1 onion, finely sliced
1 carrot, peeled and diced
2 sticks celery, trimmed and diced
4 cloves garlic, finely chopped
2 tsp dried oregano
1 tsp paprika
3 sprigs fresh rosemary, leaves picked and chopped

150ml red wine
2 x 390g cartons Italian chopped tomatoes by Sainsbury's
2 tbsp red wine vinegar
½ tsp caster sugar
400g baby aubergines, halved lengthways
150g mixed olives
500g sweet potatoes, peeled and cubed
50g feta, crumbled
Few fresh mint leaves, roughly chopped

---

1 Preheat the oven to 180°C, fan 160°C, gas 4. Heat 1 tbsp of the oil in a large shallow flameproof casserole and fry the lamb over a high heat for 2 mins each side, until browned. Remove with a slotted spoon and set aside.

2 Add the onion, carrot and celery to the casserole, and fry over a medium heat for 10 mins, adding the garlic, oregano, paprika and half the rosemary for the last min. Stir in the wine and bring to the boil, then add the tomatoes, vinegar and sugar, and cook for 1 min. Top with the lamb, cover and cook in the oven for 1 hour.

3 Meanwhile, put the aubergines, cut-side up, on a baking tray, drizzle over the rest of the oil and sprinkle over the rosemary. Bake for 30 mins, until just golden.

4 After the lamb has been cooking for 1 hour, reduce the oven temperature to 160°C, fan 140°C, gas 3. Remove the casserole from the oven and add the roasted aubergines, olives and sweet potatoes. Stir gently to coat in the sauce, re-arranging the lamb pieces back on the top. Cook, uncovered, in the oven for a further 1 hour, or until the lamb is tender and falls apart easily. Scatter over the feta and mint just before serving.

Per serving: 2478kJ/592kcal (30%), 27.6g fat (39%), 9.5g saturates (48%), 21.3g sugars (24%), 1.84g salt (31%)

SERVES 4
PREP TIME 10 mins
COOK TIME
2 hours 20 mins

Lamb with tamarind & dates

The sharp, sour taste of tamarind works beautifully with the richness of the lamb shoulder and the sweetness of the dates

767g boneless lamb shoulder joint by Sainsbury's
1 tbsp olive oil
2 red onions, cut into wedges
2 cloves garlic, chopped
1 glass red wine
1 tbsp tamarind paste by Sainsbury's

390g carton Italian chopped tomatoes by Sainsbury's
2 x 410g tins chickpeas, drained and rinsed
75g ready to eat pitted dates, chopped
Chopped fresh flat-leaf parsley and naan bread, to serve

1 Preheat the oven to 160°C, fan 140°C, gas 3. Trim any excess fat from the lamb. Heat the oil in a large flameproof casserole over a medium heat and brown the lamb all over, then transfer to a plate.

2 Add the onions to the casserole and fry for 5-6 mins until softened. Stir in the garlic and fry for 1 min. Add the wine and tamarind paste, and bubble for 2 mins. Add the tomatoes, then half fill the empty carton with water and add to the casserole.

3 Return the lamb to the casserole, then add the chickpeas and dates. Bring to the boil, cover and transfer to the oven for 2 hours or until the lamb is tender. Shred the lamb, season to taste and scatter over the parsley. Serve with the naan bread.

Per serving: 3836kJ/914kcal (46%), 36g fat (51%), 13.1g saturates (66%), 21.2g sugars (24%), 0.96g salt (16%)

Squid & chorizo casserole

A Spanish-inspired casserole served with spicy padrón peppers

500g prepared squid, from the instore fish counter, cut into 5 x 5cm pieces and scored on the inside

1 tbsp olive oil

250g pack 12 mini chorizo cooking sausages by Sainsbury's, thickly sliced

1 onion, sliced

1 red pepper, deseeded and sliced

1 yellow pepper, deseeded and sliced

3 cloves garlic, finely chopped

1 fresh bay leaf

3 fresh thyme sprigs

½ tsp smoked paprika

150ml dry sherry

2 x 390g cartons chopped tomatoes by Sainsbury's

410g tin chickpeas, drained and rinsed

500g baby potatoes, larger ones halved

135g pack padrón peppers by Sainsbury's

Handful fresh flat-leaf parsley, chopped

1   Preheat the oven to 160°C, fan 140°C, gas 3. Heat half the oil in a large ovenproof pan and cook the chorizo over a medium heat for 4-5 mins, until curled and crisp at the edges. Remove with a slotted spoon and set aside. Add the onion and peppers to the pan, and cook for 5-10 mins, until softened.

2   Stir in the garlic, bay leaf, thyme and smoked paprika. Pour in the sherry, bring to the boil and bubble rapidly for 1-2 mins. Stir in the chopped tomatoes, chickpeas, potatoes, cooked squid and 400ml water. Cover and cook in the oven for 1 hour, until the squid and potatoes are tender.

3   Just before the casserole is ready, heat the remaining oil in a frying pan and cook the padrón peppers over a high heat for 2-3 mins, turning frequently. Serve the stew, garnished with parsley, with the padrón peppers alongside.

Per serving: 2856kJ/684kcal (34%), 32g fat (46%), 9.5g saturates (48%), 17.1g sugars (19%), 3.37g salt (56%)

Cook's tip

Padrón peppers are a variety of small, mild and sweet Spanish peppers, But beware, as the odd one will have a fiery kick! Although not essential, they add a delicious authentic flavour to this Mediterranean stew.

Root vegetable bake

This recipe uses pearl barley, which is a great alternative to rice, couscous or pasta

200g pearl barley
300g fresh beetroot, scrubbed and cut into thin wedges
2 tbsp olive oil
600g butternut squash, peeled, deseeded and diced
2 red onions, thickly sliced
1 large fennel bulb, trimmed and sliced

1 parsnip, peeled, trimmed and diced
6 cloves garlic, unpeeled
Pinch of crushed chillies
1 tsp ground cumin
20g parmesan, grated
2 tbsp chopped fresh parsley
2 tbsp chopped fresh mint
Lemon wedges, to serve (optional)

1 Prepare the pearl barley according to pack instructions: drain and rinse in cold water, tip into a pan and cover with cold water, then bring to the boil and simmer for 1 hour 15 mins, until tender. Drain.

2 Meanwhile, preheat the oven to 200ºC, 180ºC fan, gas 6. Put the beetroot in a baking tray with 1 tbsp of the oil and toss to coat. Roast in the oven for 15 mins.

3 Add the butternut squash, red onion, fennel, parsnip and garlic to the beetroot. Scatter over the chillies and cumin, add the remaining oil and toss through to coat. Season to taste and roast in the oven for 30 mins, until all the vegetables are golden and tender.

4 Remove the vegetables from the oven and carefully pick out the cloves of garlic. Squeeze the flesh from the skins (discard the skins) and stir through the roasted vegetables with the pearl barley and parmesan. Scatter over the parsley and mint and serve with the lemon wedges, if using.

Per serving: 789kJ/188kcal (9%), 5.5g fat (8%), 1.3g saturates (7%), 11.8g sugars (13%), 0.16g salt (3%)

Lentil cottage pie

Our meat-free version of the ever-popular family bake

200g dried green lentils

10g dried mixed mushrooms

1.5kg Maris Piper potatoes, peeled and cut into chunks

4 tbsp semi-skimmed milk

25g unsalted butter

2 tbsp olive oil

1 onion, finely chopped

1 carrot, peeled and diced

2 sticks celery, trimmed and diced

4 cloves garlic, finely chopped

1 tsp paprika

½ tsp hot chilli powder

3 sprigs fresh rosemary, leaves picked and chopped

6 sprigs fresh thyme, chopped

1 fresh bay leaf

1 tbsp tomato purée

2 x 390g cartons Italian chopped tomatoes by Sainsbury's

200g chestnut mushrooms, thickly sliced

150ml white wine

200g baby leaf spinach or kale

25g mature Cheddar, finely grated

1 Cook the lentils according to the pack instructions: simmer in a pan of boiling water for 45 mins, then drain. Put the dried mushrooms in a heatproof bowl, then pour over 150ml boiling water and leave to soak for 10 mins. Drain, reserving the liquid, and chop the rehydrated mushrooms.

2 Put the potatoes in a large pan, cover with cold water, bring to the boil and cook for 15-20 mins, until tender. Drain and return to the pan. Add the milk and butter and mash until smooth. Set aside.

3 Meanwhile, heat 1 tbsp of the oil in a large pan. Add the onion, carrot, celery and garlic, and fry over a medium heat for 10 mins, until softened. Stir in the paprika, chilli powder, rosemary, thyme, bay leaf, tomato purée and chopped tomatoes, and cook over a gentle heat for 10-15 mins, until slightly thickened.

4 Heat the remaining oil in a large frying pan and fry the chestnut mushrooms for 5-10 mins, until golden. Stir in the rehydrated mushrooms, soaking liquid and wine. Bring to the boil, then reduce the heat and simmer for 2-3 mins. Stir in the lentils and cook for 5 mins, then stir into the vegetable and tomato mixture. Add the spinach or kale and transfer everything to a 2-litre ovenproof dish. Preheat the oven to 200°C, fan 180°C, gas 6.

5 Spoon the mashed potato over the lentil mixture and scatter over the cheese. Bake in the oven for 25 mins, until the top is golden and the filling is piping hot.

Per serving: 1745kJ/414kcal (21%), 10.1g fat (14%), 4g saturates (20%), 10.7g sugars (12%), 0.15g salt (3%)

SERVES 8
PREP TIME
15 mins, plus cooling
COOK TIME
1 hour 45 mins

Red onion & goats' cheese tart

Slow-roasting the onions elevates this vegetarian tart to something special

5 red onions, halved

8 sprigs fresh thyme, the leaves from 2 of the sprigs picked

1 whole garlic bulb, halved horizontally

2 tbsp olive oil, plus a little extra for greasing

2 tbsp balsamic vinegar

1 tbsp clear honey

350g puff pastry

Flour, for dusting

4 medium eggs, beaten

100g crème fraîche

125g goats' cheese, roughly crumbled

20g pine nuts

Wild rocket leaves, to serve

1   Preheat the oven to 180°C, fan 160°C, gas 4. Put the onions, 6 thyme sprigs and the halved garlic bulb in a small roasting tin and drizzle with the olive oil, balsamic vinegar and honey. Cover with foil and cook in the oven for 1 hour 15 mins, until tender. Remove the foil for the last 15 mins to caramelise the onions.

2   Meanwhile, roll the puff pastry out on a lightly floured surface to a 32cm diameter circle and use to line a greased 23cm round shallow cake tin. Let the excess pastry hang over the side of the tin as it will be folded into the centre of the tart when the filling has been added. Prick the pastry base all over with a fork and chill in the fridge while preparing the filling.

3   Whisk together the eggs, crème fraîche and most of the thyme leaves, and season to taste. Fold in three-quarters of the goats' cheese.

4   Discard the thyme from the tin of red onions. Squeeze the garlic cloves from their skins, roughly chop and stir into the egg mixture. Thickly slice half the onions and cut the rest into quarters. Put half the onions in the pastry case and slowly pour the egg mixture around them. Arrange the remaining onions on top. Scatter over the pine nuts and remaining cheese. Gently fold in the edges of the pastry to partially cover the filling. Put the tin on a baking sheet and bake in the oven for 25-30 mins, until the filling is set and the pastry is crisp and golden.

5   Cool for 10 mins, then carefully remove from the tin. Scatter the remaining thyme leaves over the top and serve warm with the rocket.

Per serving: 1598kJ/384kcal (19%), 25g fat (36%), 11.8g saturates (59%), 11g sugars (12%), 0.43g salt (8%)

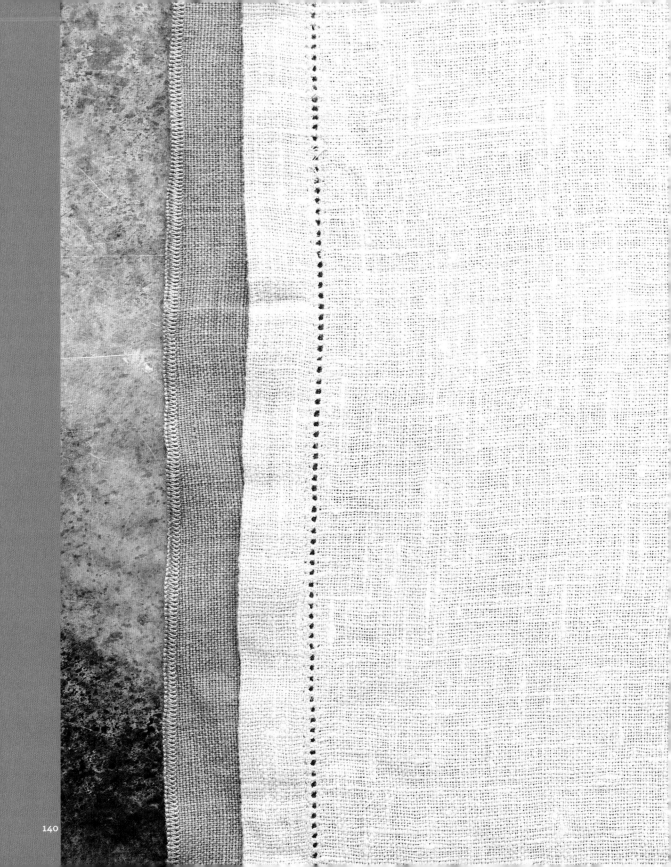

special occasions

SERVES 8
PREP TIME 25 mins
COOK TIME
1 hour 30 mins

Bonfire sausage stew

Remember, remember the 5th of November with this smoky sausage and squash stew. Great served with baked potatoes or on a bed of rice

1 tbsp olive oil
2 x 250g packs Taste the Difference ultimate outdoor-bred pork cocktail sausages
250g pack Spanish mini cooking chorizo sausages by Sainsbury's, cut into quarters
2 red onions, roughly chopped
½ tsp crushed dried chillies (optional)
1 medium butternut squash, peeled, deseeded and cut into 2cm cubes

2 tbsp black treacle
2 x 390g cartons Italian chopped tomatoes by Sainsbury's
500ml beef stock, made with 1 stock cube
2 x 150g packs Taste the Difference mixed sweet baby peppers, halved and deseeded
4 tbsp soured cream, to serve
Chopped fresh flat-leaf parsley, to serve

1 Heat the oil in a large flameproof casserole over a high heat. Add the sausages and fry until browned all over, then remove from the pan and set aside.

2 Reduce the heat to low and add the chorizo, onions and chilli (if using). Cook gently, stirring occasionally, for 10-12 mins, until the onions are soft and translucent. Stir in the squash, treacle, tomatoes and stock and bring slowly to the boil. Return the sausages to the pan and add the peppers. Partially cover the pan and simmer for 1 hour until the squash is tender.

3 Serve garnished with a spoonful of the soured cream and the parsley.

Per serving: 1080kJ/259kcal (13%), 16g fat (23%), 5.4g saturates (27%), 13.5g sugars (15%), 1.88g salt (31%)

Bacon baked potatoes

Bake 4 Taste the Difference Vivaldi baking potatoes in an oven heated to 200°C, fan 180°C, gas 6 for 1 hour. Grill 2 rashers bacon until crisp; cut into strips. Mix with 50g baby leaf spinach and 75g grated Cheddar. Make a cross in each potato and fill with the bacon mixture. Pop under a hot grill and grill until the cheese is melted and bubbling. Season with pepper.

Serves 4 Prep time: 10 mins Cook time: 1 hour 10 mins
Per serving: 1542kJ/366kcal (18%), 8.8g fat (13%), 4.9g saturates (25%), 4.3g sugars (5%), 0.69g salt (12%)

Risotto-stuffed mini squash

Creamy risotto served in a roasted squash is a brilliant dish to serve at a Bonfire Night celebration, or on any other chilly evening

4 harlequin squash

1 tbsp olive oil

4 rashers dry-cured streaky bacon, chopped

1 small onion, finely chopped

300g peeled and cubed butternut squash

1 clove garlic, chopped

1 tbsp chopped fresh thyme leaves

200g arborio risotto rice

750-900ml hot vegetable stock, made using 1 stock cube

Knob of butter

FOR THE THYME GREMOLATA

1 clove garlic, finely chopped

1 tbsp fresh thyme leaves

Zest of 1 small lemon

1 Preheat the oven to 200°C, fan 180°C, gas 6. Using a sharp knife, cut the top off each squash and level the bottom. Using a spoon, scoop out the seeds and discard. Bake the squash on an oiled baking tray for 50-60 mins, or until tender.

2 Heat the oil in a large shallow pan and fry the bacon for 3-4 mins, or until crisp. Remove from the pan and drain on kitchen paper. Add the onion to the pan and cook for 6-7 mins, until beginning to soften.

3 Add the cubed squash to the pan with the garlic and thyme. Gently cook for 5 mins, stirring now and then. Turn up the heat, tip in the rice and stir to coat. Cook for 1-2 mins.

4 Meanwhile, heat the stock in a separate pan and bring to a simmer over a low heat. Add a couple of ladlefuls of hot stock to the rice and simmer, stirring, until the stock has been absorbed. Gradually add the remaining stock, a ladleful at a time, until the rice is tender and creamy – this should take about 20 mins.

5 Stir in the butter and bacon, then fill each hot baked squash with the risotto. Mix together the ingredients for the thyme gremolata and sprinkle over the top of the squash to serve.

Per serving: 2234kJ/531kcal (27%), 13.2g fat (19%), 4.7g saturates (24%), 24g sugars (27%), 1.77g salt (30%)

Toffee apples

Apples are in season so make the most of them with crunchy toffee apples. They are super-easy to make and you can use any eating apple you like

8 wooden lollipop sticks or skewers
8 small eating apples
225g light brown soft sugar
125g golden syrup

½ tbsp white wine vinegar
15g unsalted butter
Sunflower oil, for greasing
3 ginger snap biscuits, crushed (optional)

1   Push a skewer into each apple through the stalk end and set aside.

2   Put the sugar, syrup and vinegar in a heavy-based pan with 2 tbsp water and heat gently, without stirring, until the sugar has dissolved. You may need to swirl the pan a little, but don't be tempted to use a spoon.

3   Once the sugar has dissolved, increase the heat to medium-high and boil until the syrup is deep golden brown and reaches the 'hard crack' stage, which is 150°C on a sugar thermometer. If you don't have a sugar thermometer, drizzle a little of the toffee from a fork into a bowl of cold water. If it sets to brittle threads immediately, it's ready; if it's still soft, it needs a little more cooking. Remove from the heat and stir in the butter.

4   Working quickly, dip each apple into the toffee, tilting the pan and twirling the apples to get an even coating. Allow the excess to drip back into the pan, then place each apple on a lightly oiled plate, sprinkle the apples with the crushed ginger biscuits (if using) and leave to set.

Per toffee apple: 1093kJ/258kcal (13%), 3g fat (4%), 1.3g saturates (7%), 53.9g sugars (60%), 0.16g salt (3%)

Parkin

The orange zest isn't traditional and may even have Yorkshiremen up in arms but it adds a lovely zestiness to this rich sticky cake usually served on Bonfire Night

200g unsalted butter, plus extra for greasing
125g black treacle
150g golden syrup
225g self-raising flour
100g medium oatmeal
75g light brown soft sugar

2 tsp ground ginger
¾ tsp ground nutmeg
Zest of 1 orange
3 tbsp semi-skimmed milk
1 large egg, beaten

1   Preheat the oven to 160°C, fan 140°C, gas 3. Grease and line a 20cm square tin.

2   Melt the butter, black treacle and golden syrup in a small pan over a low heat.

3   Meanwhile, stir together the flour, oatmeal, brown sugar, ginger and nutmeg in a large bowl.

4   Pour the butter and treacle mixture into the dry ingredients and gently mix together using a balloon whisk. Whisk in the orange zest and milk, then add the egg and mix to combine.

5   Pour into the prepared tin and bake for 50 mins to 1 hour, until firm to the touch. Leave to cool in the tin before turning out.

6   Once cool, cut into 20 squares.

Per square: 827kJ/197kcal (10%), 9.3g fat (13%), 5.2g saturates (26%), 14.4g sugars (16%), 0.18g salt (3%)

Cook's tip
This parkin will become softer and stickier if you wrap it in greaseproof paper, then in foil, and store in a cool place for several days before serving.

SERVES 8
PREP TIME
35 mins, plus chilling and cooling
COOK TIME
1 hour 40 mins

Pumpkin pie

A Thanksgiving classic in America, try serving it up at a Halloween party

375g prepared pumpkin or squash flesh, cut into 2-3cm chunks

500g block shortcrust pastry by Sainsbury's

250ml evaporated milk

1 large egg, plus 1 egg yolk

125g dark brown soft sugar

2 tbsp maple syrup

2 tsp plain flour

1½ tsp vanilla extract

1½ tsp mixed spice

Pinch ground allspice

Milk, for brushing

1 Steam the squash or pumpkin over a pan of boiling water for 20 mins, until very tender. Remove from the heat and set aside to cool.

2 On a lightly floured surface, roll out 400g of the pastry, until it's big enough to fill a 20cm fluted tart tin at least 4cm deep with some overlap. Use to line the tin. Leave any excess hanging above the edge as the pastry will shrink slightly when baked. Roll out the remaining pastry and, using a sharp knife or cutters, cut out a few leaf shapes. Put on a baking sheet and chill with the tart case in the fridge for 30 mins, until firm. Put a baking sheet in the oven and preheat the oven to 200°C, fan 180°C, gas 6.

3 Prick the base of the chilled pastry case with a fork, line with a sheet of crumpled greaseproof paper and fill with baking beans (or rice or lentils). Bake on the preheated baking sheet for 15 mins, then remove the paper and beans and bake for a further 10 mins, until the pastry is cooked and slightly sandy to the touch.

4 Meanwhile, put the cooled steamed squash and the remaining ingredients except for the milk in a blender (or use a jug and a hand blender) and blend until smooth. Pour into the pie case. Reduce the oven temperature to 180°C, fan 160°C, gas 4 and bake for 50-55 mins, until the filling is just set. When the tart has 20 mins' cooking time remaining, brush the pastry leaves with a little of the milk and bake in the oven alongside the tart.

5 Remove from the oven and let the tart and leaves cool completely, then transfer to the fridge to chill for a few hours or overnight. Trim the excess pastry from the tart and, just before serving, top with the leaves.

Per serving: 1966kJ/470kcal (24%), 23.8g fat (34%), 11.5g saturates (58%), 24.1g sugars (27%), 0.22g salt (4%)

SERVES
6 with leftovers
PREP TIME 20 mins
plus resting
COOK TIME
2 hours 20 mins

Roasted stuffed goose

A great alternative to turkey on the Christmas table

3kg oven-ready goose, giblets removed

1 onion, peeled and halved

Steamed kale, to serve

FOR THE PEAR & CHESTNUT STUFFING

2 Conference pears, peeled, cored and cubed

100g cooked chestnuts, crumbled

75g dried cherries

105g pack Italian smoked pancetta
by Sainsbury's, finely diced

1 egg, lightly beaten

1   Preheat the oven to 220°C, fan 200°C, gas 7. Make the stuffing. In a bowl, mix
    together all the stuffing ingredients until well combined. Season and set aside.

2   Pat the goose dry with kitchen towel, then prick the skin all over. Season inside
    and out with salt and freshly ground black pepper, and put the onion in the
    cavity. Spoon the stuffing into the neck end, tuck the neck flap around the
    stuffing and pat to make a rounded shape. Secure with cocktail sticks; set aside.

3   Transfer the goose to a roasting rack in a roasting tin. Roast for 20 mins, then
    reduce the temperature to 180°C, fan 160°C, gas 4 and roast for a further 2 hours,
    basting with the pan juices, until the goose is cooked. To check it's cooked, insert a
    skewer into the thickest part of the thigh to see if the juices run clear.

4   Cover loosely with foil and let rest for 10 mins. Carve and serve with the kale.

Per serving (150g goose with kale): 3164kJ/758kcal (38%), 42.5g fat (61%),
3.5g saturates (18%), 18.8g sugars (21%), 1.26g salt (21%)

Pork & prune stuffing

Soak 100g pitted prunes in 50ml Madeira for at least
8 hours. Chop the prunes and mix with 400g pork
sausagemeat, the Madeira, a handful of breadcrumbs
and 1 tbsp chopped fresh thyme. Season to taste. Use
this stuffing as an alternative to the one above to
stuff the goose, if you like, or shape into balls and
bake at 180°C, fan 160°C, gas 4 for 25 mins.

Serves 4 Prep time: 5 mins plus soaking Cook time: 25 mins
Per stuffing ball: 490kJ/118kcal (6%), 7.5g fat (11%),
2.7g saturates (14%), 3.3g sugars (4%), 0.49g salt (8%)

Whole glazed gammon

A celebration ham that will look stunning on a Boxing Day buffet

1 large unsmoked boneless gammon joint
(approximately 3kg)
1 litre cloudy apple juice
2 onions, peeled and halved
2 fresh bay leaves
2 whole star anise
20 black peppercorns

FOR THE GLAZE
1 tbsp English mustard powder
3 tbsp Bramley apple sauce
2 tbsp light brown soft sugar

6 whole star anise

FOR THE WALDORF SALAD
3 little gem lettuce, leaves separated
75g bag SO organic watercress
35g sultanas
4 sticks celery, trimmed and sliced
40g walnut halves, lightly toasted
(see Cook's tip)
1 red eating apple, cored and thinly sliced
4 tbsp honey and mustard dressing
by Sainsbury's

1   Put the gammon in a large pan with the apple juice, onions, bay leaves, star anise and peppercorns; add just enough water to cover the gammon. Bring to the boil, reduce the heat to low and simmer for 1 hour 30 mins, or if your gammon is a different weight calculate the cooking time allowing 15 mins per 500g.

2   Preheat the oven to 220°C, fan 200°C, gas 7. Lift the gammon from the poaching liquid (cool, then freeze the liquid and use in soups). Remove any string and use a sharp knife to cut away the skin, leaving behind a good layer of fat.

3   Score the fat in a diamond pattern then sprinkle over the mustard powder and pat it in. Spread the apple sauce over the mustard then sprinkle over the sugar. Press the star anise into the top of the gammon at evenly spaced intervals. Put on a roasting tray lined with foil and bake for 30-35 mins until the glaze is golden.

4   Meanwhile, for the Waldorf salad, toss together all the ingredients in a large bowl. Season to taste and serve with thick sliced of the gammon.

Per serving (150g gammon, plus salad): 1721kJ/409kcal (21%), 12.8g fat (18%), 3.6g saturates (18%), 24.2g sugars (27%), 4.24g salt (71%)

Cook's tip
To toast nuts, heat a dry frying pan over a high heat, add the nuts and toast, shaking the pan, for 2-3 mins.

SERVES 6-8
PREP TIME 10 mins,
plus resting
COOK TIME 2 hours
30 mins, plus resting

Peppered roast beef

This flavoursome rib of beef is perfect for a Boxing Day lunch

2.5-3kg rib of beef (with 2 bones)
2 tbsp mixed peppercorns

2 tsp Dijon mustard
1 large onion, thickly sliced into rings

1   Remove the joint from the fridge and bring to room temperature. Preheat the
    oven to 200°C, fan 180°C, gas 6. Weigh the joint and calculate the cooking time.
    Allow 15 mins per 450g, plus 15 mins for rare, or 20 mins per 450g plus 20 mins
    for medium. Lightly crush the peppercorns with a pestle and mortar. Brush the
    mustard over the beef and season all over with salt.

2   Press the crushed peppercorns all over the beef, patting them in firmly. Arrange
    the sliced onion in a single layer in the centre of a roasting tray and put the beef
    – with the bones on the underside – on the onions.

3   Roast the beef for 30 mins, then reduce the heat to 160°C, fan 140°C, gas 3
    and roast for the remaining calculated time.

4   Remove from the oven, cover and let rest in a warm place for 20 mins before
    carving and serving with the hot and sour cabbage (see below), if liked.

Per serving (150g beef): 1531kJ/365kcal (18%), 17.3g fat (25%),
7.7g saturates (39%), 1.2g sugars (1%), 0.31g salt (5%)

Hot & sour cabbage

Pare the zest of 2 oranges, then halve and juice both.
Add the zest and juice to a pan with 1 shredded red
cabbage, 2 deseeded and sliced red chillies, 10 lightly
crushed juniper berries, 75g butter, 3 tbsp light brown
soft sugar and 3 tbsp red wine vinegar. Season to taste,
cover and cook on a low heat for 1 hour. Remove the
lid, increase the heat to medium and cook for 30 mins.

Serves 4 Prep time: 10 mins Cook time: 1 hour 30 mins
Per serving: 1044kJ/251kcal (13%), 16.2g fat (23%),
9.3g saturates (47%), 20.1g sugars (22%), 0.04g salt (1%)

SERVES 6 plus leftovers
PREP TIME 30-35 mins, plus resting
COOK TIME 4 hours 10 mins

Lamb shoulder with boulangère potatoes

A crowd-pleasing roast to serve on a wintry weekend – this recipe will give you some delicious leftovers to use up during the week, too

2kg lamb shoulder joint by Sainsbury's
1 bulb garlic, broken into cloves and peeled
12 anchovy fillets
1.8kg Maris Piper potatoes, peeled and very thinly sliced
3 onions, finely sliced
4 sprigs fresh rosemary, leaves picked and chopped
6 sprigs fresh thyme, leaves picked
500ml chicken stock, made with ½ stock cube
200g fine beans
200g kale, shredded

Small handful fresh mint leaves, chopped
20g toasted flaked almonds

FOR THE RED WINE GRAVY
125ml red wine
400ml lamb stock, made with ½ stock cube
1 tbsp redcurrant jelly
1 tbsp balsamic vinegar
3 fresh thyme sprigs
1 fresh bay leaf
1 tbsp cornflour, blended to a smooth paste with 1 tbsp water

1   Preheat the oven to 150°C, fan 130°C, gas 2. Cut 12 deep slits into the lamb and stuff each with 1 garlic clove and 1 anchovy fillet. Layer the potatoes, onions, rosemary and thyme in a large roasting tin (about 24cm x 34cm x 6cm), seasoning lightly between each layer. Pour over the stock and place the lamb on top.

2   Roast in the oven for 4 hours, until the lamb is tender and the potatoes are golden. If the potatoes begin to overbrown, cover the tin with foil. Remove from the oven, cover with foil (if not covered) and rest for 20 mins.

3   While the lamb is resting, make the gravy. Pour the wine into a small pan with the stock, redcurrant jelly, vinegar, thyme and bay leaf. Heat gently for 3-4 mins, until the jelly has dissolved. Whisk in the cornflour paste and slowly bring to the boil, stirring, until just thickened. Simmer for a further 2-3 mins.

4   Cook the beans and kale in a pan of boiling water for 3-4 mins. Drain and transfer to a serving dish with the mint and almonds. Season to taste. Carve the lamb and serve with the boulangère potatoes, minted beans and kale, and red wine gravy.

Per serving (150g lamb with vegetables): 2927kJ/697kcal (35%), 24.4g fat (35%), 9.9g saturates (50%), 8.6g sugars (10%), 2.17g salt (36%)

SERVES 6
PREP TIME
30 mins, plus resting
COOK TIME 2 hours
10 mins

Mushroom & pine nut stuffed leg of lamb

This luxurious boneless roast is a real crowd-pleaser. It looks spectacular, too, so take it to the table to carve

50g pine nuts

50g dried porcini mushrooms

1 tbsp olive oil

250g closed cup chestnut mushrooms, thinly sliced

4 cloves garlic, crushed

Small handful fresh thyme, roughly chopped

Large handful fresh flat-leaf parsley, leaves picked and roughly chopped

Zest of 1 lemon

2kg leg of lamb from the instore counter, boned and butterflied

Zest of 1 lemon

Steamed carrots and broccoli, to serve

1 Preheat the oven to 180°C, fan 160°C, gas 4. Toast the pine nuts in a dry frying pan over a medium heat for 2-3 mins, then remove from the pan and set aside to cool. Put the dried porcini mushrooms in a heatproof bowl and pour over enough boiling water to cover. Leave to soak for 10 mins.

2 Heat the oil in the frying pan and fry the chestnut mushrooms over a medium heat for 4-5 mins, stirring occasionally, until tender. Add the garlic and fry for a further 1-2 mins, until the mushrooms are deep golden. Set aside to cool.

3 Drain and roughly chop the soaked porcini, discarding the soaking liquid. Stir into the fried mushrooms with the thyme, parsley, lemon zest and toasted pine nuts.

4 Lay the butterflied lamb out on a board and season both sides with freshly ground black pepper. Spread the mushroom mixture in an even layer over the meat. Starting at one end, roll the lamb up tightly, as if it were a Swiss roll, tucking in any sticking-out edges and pushing the filling in as you go. Tie tightly with kitchen string at 3-4 intervals to keep the joint neatly together.

5 Put the stuffed lamb, seam-side down, in a roasting tin. Roast, uncovered, for 1 hour 45 mins, until golden brown and cooked through. Baste once or twice with the pan juices during cooking. Remove from the oven and cover the lamb with foil. Leave to rest for 20 mins before serving with the steamed vegetables.

Per serving (150g lamb with vegetables): 1924kJ/460kcal (23%), 22.8g fat (33%), 5.9g saturates (30%), 5.4g sugars (6%), 0.35g salt (6%)

Side of salmon with horseradish crust

Bring something special to the Christmas table with this impressive salmon dish served with roasted root veg

---

500g bunch fresh beetroot, trimmed, peeled and cut into wedges

2 tbsp olive oil, plus extra for greasing

Leaves from 8 sprigs fresh thyme

Small handful fresh dill, chopped

50g fresh white breadcrumbs

Zest of 1 lemon

25g unsalted butter, melted

720g side of salmon, scaled and pin-boned

5 tsp creamed horseradish

500g pack Chantenay carrots, halved lengthways

1 tbsp maple syrup

Watercress, to garnish (optional)

---

1 Preheat the oven to 200°C, fan 180°C, gas 6. Put the beetroot in a small shallow roasting dish with 1 tbsp of the oil and half of the thyme leaves. Season to taste and toss together so the beetroot is coated in the oil. Cover the dish tightly with foil and put on the middle shelf of the oven. Bake for 50 mins until tender.

2 Meanwhile, line a baking tray with foil and brush lightly with the extra oil. Mix the chopped dill with the breadcrumbs, lemon zest, melted butter and season to taste. Place the salmon, skin-side down, on the oiled foil and spread the horseradish over the flesh in an even layer. Top with the breadcrumb mix, pressing it down gently, then set aside.

3 Put the carrots in a separate small baking tray with the remaining oil and thyme leaves, and the maple syrup. Season with freshly ground black pepper and toss together. Set aside.

4 After the beetroot has been in the oven for 30 mins, transfer the carrots and salmon to the oven - ideally placing the carrots alongside the beetroot and the salmon on the top shelf above - and roast for 20 mins, until the crumb coating is golden and the salmon is cooked through, opaque and flakes easily.

5 Toss the beetroot and carrots together. Garnish the salmon with watercress, if using, and serve with the beetroot and carrots.

Per serving: 1683kJ/403kcal (20%), 21.5g fat (31%), 6.3g saturates (32%), 14.2g sugars (16%), 0.69g salt (12%)

SERVES 4
PREP TIME 30 mins
COOK TIME 35 mins

Monkfish in Parma ham with warm tomato salsa

An elegant dish that's ideal for dinner parties or a Christmas Eve supper

2 x 350g whole monkfish tails, skin, bone
and fine membrane removed
8 slices Parma ham
200g shredded kale, steamed, to serve

FOR THE WARM TOMATO SALSA
800g ripe vine tomatoes
2 tbsp cold-pressed rapeseed oil
2 cloves garlic, finely chopped
1 tsp ground coriander
1 tsp dried oregano
1 tbsp sherry vinegar

1. Preheat the oven to 200°C, fan 180°C, gas 6. Make the salsa. Score a cross in the base of each tomato, put in a heatproof bowl and cover with boiling water. Leave for 1 min, then drain and refresh in cold water. Peel and discard the skins, halve the tomatoes and discard the seeds. Chop the flesh and set aside. Heat the oil in a pan over a low heat and cook the garlic for 1-2 mins. Increase the heat to high and add the coriander, oregano, tomatoes and vinegar. Cook on a high heat, stirring, for 5-10 mins, until the tomatoes start to reduce. Season to taste.

2. Wrap the ham around the monkfish. Spoon the salsa into a roasting dish, and top with the fish. Roast for 18-20 mins, until the fish is cooked through. Serve sliced with the tomato salsa, steamed kale and cauliflower mash (see below), if liked.

Per serving (without cauliflower mash): 1118kJ/267kcal (13%), 11.7g fat (17%), 2.2g saturates (11%), 7.2g sugars (8%), 1.23g salt (21%)

Creamy cauliflower mash

Break 1 head cauliflower into florets, put in a pan and cover with 1 litre whole milk. Add 1 fresh bay leaf and a sprinkling of ground nutmeg. Cover and simmer for 30-35 mins, until tender. Drain and mash. Stir in 25g butter and 60g grated parmesan. Season to taste and serve sprinkled with extra nutmeg and drizzled with 2-3 tsp truffle oil.

Serves 4 Prep time: 10 mins Cook time: 35 mins
Per serving: 721kJ/174kcal (9%), 13.4g fat (19%), 6.8g saturates (34%), 2.9g sugars (3%), 0.28g salt (5%)

MAKES 8
PREP TIME
30 mins, plus proving
and cooling
COOK TIME
25-30 mins

Mini panettones

A twist on the Italian festive favourite and alternative to mince pies

90ml semi-skimmed milk	Zest of 1 orange
40g caster sugar	Zest of 1 lemon
2 sachets fast action dried yeast	Pinch of salt
4 medium eggs; 1 separated	1 tsp freshly grated nutmeg
1 tsp vanilla extract	50g glacé cherries, halved
150g unsalted butter, softened	150g dried mixed fruit by Sainsbury's
300g strong white flour	80ml dark rum

1   Line a muffin tin with 8 muffin cases. Pour the milk into a small bowl and leave to come to room temperature. Stir in a quarter of the sugar and all the yeast, until dissolved. Set aside until it starts to froth. Meanwhile, in a small bowl, whisk together the 3 whole eggs, the egg yolk and the vanilla. Set aside.

2   In a large mixing bowl, beat together the butter and remaining sugar until pale and creamy. Slowly add the egg mixture, beating well with each addition. If the mixture starts to curdle, add 50g of the flour and continue until all the egg is incorporated. Stir in the citrus zests, then sift in the flour, salt and nutmeg. Pour in the yeast mixture and use a spatula to slowly mix together. The dough will be very sticky - somewhere between a regular dough and a cake mix in consistency.

3   On a very well floured surface, tip out the dough, and knead for 10 mins until smooth. Transfer to a large bowl, cover with cling film and leave in a warm place to rise for 1 hour. Meanwhile, soak all the fruit in the rum.

4   When the dough has risen, tip onto a floured surface. Knead for 1 min, then knead in the fruit until evenly distributed. Divide the dough into 8, shape into smooth balls and put 1 in each muffin case. Cover loosely with cling film. Leave in a warm place until the dough has risen above the top of the cases - this will take about 30-45 mins. Preheat the oven to 200°C, fan 180°C, gas 6.

5   Brush the tops with the egg white and bake for 15 mins. Reduce the temperature to 180°C, fan 160°C, gas 5 and bake for 10-15 mins until risen and golden and a skewer inserted into the centre comes out clean. Cool in the tin for 15 mins, then transfer to a wire rack to cool completely.

Per panettone: 1720kJ/411kcal (21%), 18.8g fat (27%), 10.4g saturates (52%), 22.4g sugars (25%), 0.33g salt (6%)

Chocolate & pear cake

A stunning cake for Christmas, New Year or a Bonfire Night party

100g dark chocolate (minimum 70% cocoa solids), finely chopped

100ml strong freshly brewed espresso (or 1½ tbsp instant espresso powder dissolved in 100ml boiling water)

175g unsalted butter, softened, plus extra for greasing

250g light muscovado sugar

3 large eggs, at room temperature

150ml buttermilk

2 tsp vanilla extract

125g ground almonds

200g plain flour

1 tsp bicarbonate of soda

1 tsp baking powder

FOR THE PEARS

125g caster sugar

25g unsalted butter

Large pinch of sea salt flakes

4 small Conference pears, peeled, halved and cored

1   Preheat the oven to 180°C, fan 160°C, gas 4. Grease and line a deep (at least 10cm in height), 20cm loose-based cake tin, so the paper sits slightly higher than the edge of the tin. For the pears, put the sugar in a pan and place over a medium heat until it melts to a caramel – this should take about 5-7 mins. Shake the pan occasionally but do not stir. Once melted, add the butter and sea salt flakes and stir until it comes together to a smooth sauce. Pour over the base of the prepared cake tin and arrange 7 of the pear halves, cut-side down, in the caramel. Finely chop the remaining pear and set aside.

2   Put the chocolate in a small bowl and pour over the hot espresso, stirring to melt. Set aside. In a large mixing bowl whisk together the butter and sugar with an electric whisk until pale and very fluffy. Whisk in the eggs, one at a time, then the buttermilk, vanilla and, finally, the melted espresso chocolate.

3   Add the almonds to the cake mix, then sift in the flour, bicarbonate of soda and baking powder. Use a large metal spoon to gently fold the mixture together, then stir in the chopped pear half. Pour the batter into the cake tin over the pears, smooth the top and bake for 1 hour to 1 hour 10 mins, until a skewer inserted into the middle comes out clean.

4   Leave until almost cool in the tin before inverting and turning out onto a wire rack (so the pears are on the top). Transfer to a cake plate and serve warm or cold.

Per serving: 2423kJ/579kcal (29%), 30.4g fat (43%), 14g saturates (70%), 25.4g sugars (28%), 0.58g salt (10%)

SERVES 16
PREP TIME
35 mins, plus cooling
COOK TIME 30-40
mins, plus cooling

Triple chocolate gateau

A show-stopping cake that's perfect for birthdays and other celebrations

75g cocoa powder
250g unsalted butter, diced, at room temperature
500g light brown soft sugar
4 large eggs, lightly beaten
400g self-raising flour
½ tsp baking powder

FOR THE GANACHE
150g dark chocolate, grated
125ml whipping cream

TO ASSEMBLE
300ml whipping cream, softly whipped
40g white chocolate, grated
40g dark chocolate, grated
White and dark chocolate shards,
to decorate

1   Preheat the oven to 180ºC, fan 160ºC, gas 4. Grease 3 x 20cm loose bottomed round cake tins and line the bases. Put the cocoa powder, butter and sugar in a large bowl and pour over 300ml boiling water from the kettle, whisking with a balloon whisk, until the butter has melted and the sugar has dissolved.

2   Gradually whisk in the eggs, then sift in the flour and baking powder, and stir to combine. Divide evenly between the prepared cake tins and bake for 30-40 mins, until a skewer inserted in the middle comes out clean. Leave the cakes to cool in the tins.

3   To make the ganache, heat the cream in a pan and bring just to the boil. Put the grated chocolate in a heatproof bowl. Pour the hot cream over the chocolate and whisk until smooth and combined. Set aside until the ganache is cooled and is the consistency of soft butter.

4   To assemble the gateau, remove the cooled cakes from the tins and peel off the lining papers. Place one cake on a serving plate or cake stand and spread over one-third of the ganache. Scatter over one-third of the grated dark and white chocolate and top with one-third of the whipped cream. Repeat with the remaining cakes, ganache, chocolate and cream. Decorate with the chocolate shards.

Per serving: 2310kJ/553kcal (28%), 31.6g fat (45%), 18.7g saturates (94%), 39.7g sugars (44%), 0.27g salt (5%)

desserts

SERVES 4
PREP TIME 10 mins
COOK TIME
20-25 mins

Roast pears with cardamom butter

Pears are plentiful in the winter months and they taste amazing when roasted in an aromatic butter and lemon sauce

4 firm pears (such as Conference), peeled, halved and cored (larger ones cut into quarters)
50g soft unsalted butter

50g light brown soft sugar
Seeds of 8 cardamom pods, crushed
Zest of 1 lemon and juice of ½ lemon
Greek-style natural yogurt, to serve

1   Preheat the oven to 200°C, fan 180°C, gas 6. Arrange the pears in a large shallow roasting tin.

2   In a bowl, beat together the butter, sugar, crushed cardamom seeds and lemon zest until combined, then dot all over the pears. Roast in the oven for 20-25 mins, turning and basting with the juices halfway through.

3   Remove the pears from the oven, then squeeze over the lemon juice. Serve warm or cold, with spoonfuls of the yogurt.

Per serving: 1111kJ/265kcal (13%), 12.8g fat (18%), 7.4g saturates (37%), 36g sugars (40%), 0.05g salt (1%)

Cook's tip
Once you've mastered this recipe, try it with different flavoured butters. Cinnamon works a treat, as does ginger. For something a little more unusual, try some fresh thyme leaves.

Apple, elderflower & oat crumble

Crumbles make fantastic winter puds and this one uses Bramley apples and elderflower with a crunchy seed topping

900g Bramley cooking apples, peeled, cored and thickly sliced
50g light brown soft sugar
4 tbsp Taste the Difference English elderflower cordial
Zest of 1 lemon

150g self-raising flour
100g unsalted butter, chilled and cubed
50g rolled oats
75g demerara sugar
1 tbsp pumpkin seeds
1 tbsp sunflower seeds

1   Preheat the oven to 190°C, fan 170°C, gas 5. Place the apples in a large pan with the brown sugar and elderflower cordial. Cook gently over a medium heat for 4-5 mins, until the apples are just beginning to soften, stirring occasionally. Stir in the lemon zest and transfer to a 1.5-litre baking dish.

2   Sift the flour into a bowl, add the butter and rub in with your fingertips until the mixture resembles coarse breadcrumbs. Stir in the oats, demerara sugar, pumpkin and sunflower seeds, then sprinkle the mixture over the apples to cover, pressing down gently. Bake for 40-45 mins, until the crumble topping is crisp and golden.

Per serving: 2686kJ/640kcal (32%), 26.2g fat (37%), 13.1g saturates (66%), 53.8g sugars (60%), 0.31g salt (5%)

Iced forest fruits with warm white chocolate sauce ⓥ

Tip 350g frozen Black Forest fruits by Sainsbury's into a wide, shallow microwave-safe dish. Heat on 'defrost' for 3-4 mins, until semi-thawed. Meanwhile, break up 150g white chocolate and melt with 100ml double cream in a heatproof bowl set over a pan of simmering water, making sure the base of the bowl doesn't touch the water. Spoon the fruits between 4 glasses and pour over the warm chocolate sauce.

Serves 4 Prep time: 2 mins Cook time: 8 mins
Per serving: 1456kJ/350kcal (18%), 26.2g fat (37%), 16.4g saturates (82%), 25.3g sugars (28%), 0.10g salt (2%)

SERVES 8
PREP TIME
20 mins, plus chilling
COOK TIME
45-50 mins
V

Freeform plum & blueberry pie

Crisp pastry filled with luscious blueberries and plums - what a treat!

600g plums, destoned and quartered
400g fresh blueberries
125g caster sugar, plus an extra 2 tbsp
for sprinkling
2 tbsp cornflour
½ tsp ground cinnamon

FOR THE PASTRY
250g plain flour, plus extra for dusting
50g icing sugar
125g unsalted butter, chilled and diced,
plus extra for greasing
1 medium egg, beaten
2 tbsp semi-skimmed milk

1   Make the pastry. Sift the flour and icing sugar into the bowl of a food processor and add the butter. Pulse until the mixture resembles fine breadcrumbs. Pour in the egg and 1-2 tbsp ice-cold water and pulse until the mixture forms large clumps. Turn out onto a floured surface and gather the clumps together, kneading lightly to form a smooth ball. Wrap in cling film and chill in the fridge for 20 mins.

2   Roll out the pastry on a sheet of baking paper to a 40cm x 3mm thick circle, leaving the edges uneven. Transfer to a baking sheet (still on the paper). Chill in the fridge for a further 20 mins. Preheat the oven to 200°C, fan 180°C, gas 6.

3   Toss the plums, blueberries, sugar, cornflour and cinnamon together in a large bowl. Pile on top of the pastry, leaving a 6-8cm border. Gently fold in the pastry border to partially enclose the fruit. Brush the pastry edges with the milk and sprinkle with the extra sugar. Bake for 45-50 mins, until the pastry is golden and the filling is hot and bubbling.

Per serving: 1785kJ/425kcal (21%), 21g fat (14.9%), 8.4g saturates (42%), 37.4g sugars (42%), 0.04g salt (1%)

Cook's tip
This pastry needs to be handled lightly with cold hands and chilled before and after rolling. You can make it a day ahead and chill in the fridge. It will be firm, so remove from the fridge 20 mins before rolling.

Black Forest roulade

Retro flavours are given a modern makeover in a delicious roulade

150g dark chocolate (at least 70% cocoa solids), broken into small pieces

5 large eggs, separated

150g caster sugar

1 tbsp cocoa powder, plus extra for dusting

300ml double cream

125g pack Taste the Difference morello cherries with kirsch

Icing sugar, for dusting

Fresh cherries, to serve

1   Preheat the oven to 180°C, fan 160°C, gas 4. Lightly grease and line a 35cm x 24cm Swiss roll tin or shallow baking tray.

2   Melt the chocolate in a heatproof bowl set over a pan of simmering water, taking care to not let the base of the bowl touch the water. Remove from the heat and set aside to cool for 10 mins.

3   Put the egg yolks and caster sugar in a large bowl and whisk for 5-6 mins with an electric whisk, until the mixture is very thick, pale and creamy. Whisk in the melted chocolate and 1 tbsp hot water.

4   In a separate bowl, whisk the egg whites to stiff peaks. Using a metal spoon, beat 2 tbsp of the egg whites into the chocolate mixture to loosen it slightly, then gently fold in the rest of the egg whites, until thoroughly incorporated. Pour the mixture into the prepared tin and tilt the tin so the mixture reaches the corners. Bake for 20-25 mins, until risen and just firm to the touch. Remove from the oven and let cool in the tin for 5 mins.

5   Sift the 1 tbsp cocoa powder over a large sheet of baking paper and invert the warm roulade onto the paper. Remove the tin (leaving the lining paper on) and cover the roulade with a clean damp tea towel. Leave until cold.

6   In a bowl, whip the cream to soft peaks. Remove the tea towel and lining paper from the cold roulade. Spread the cream over the roulade and scatter over the cherries with kirsch. Using the paper as a guide, roll up the roulade from one short end – don't worry if it cracks a little. Transfer to a serving platter (seam-side down). Dust the roulade with the extra cocoa powder and the icing sugar and serve with the fresh cherries.

Per serving: 1518kJ/365kcal (18%), 24.4g fat (35%), 14.4g saturates (72%), 26.3g sugars (29%), 0.17g salt (3%)

Steamed blood orange pudding

A warming, comforting pud made with seasonal blood oranges. They're only around for a short time in late winter, so if you can't get hold of any, use regular oranges instead

175g unsalted butter, softened, plus extra for greasing
175g caster sugar
Zest of 1 orange
1 tsp vanilla extract
3 medium eggs, lightly beaten

175g self-raising flour
1 tsp baking powder
2 tbsp semi-skimmed milk
8 tbsp fine-cut marmalade
1 blood orange, cut into 6 thin slices
Warm custard, to serve

1   Thoroughly grease a 1.2-litre pudding basin with the extra butter. Put the softened butter and the sugar in a bowl and beat together until pale and creamy. Beat in the orange zest and vanilla extract, then gradually beat in the eggs.

2   Sift over the self-raising flour and baking powder and fold into the creamed mixture with the milk. Spoon the marmalade into the base and brush halfway up the sides of the pudding basin. Arrange the blood orange slices on top of the marmalade at the base and sides.

3   Gently spoon the sponge mixture on top of the orange slices and level the surface. Cover with a buttered double square of kitchen foil, making a pleat across the centre, and tie with string.

4   Put the pudding basin in a steamer set over simmering water and steam for 2 hours until a skewer inserted through the foil into the centre of the pudding comes out clean. If you don't have a steamer, place the pudding basin in a large pan on a trivet or upturned saucer. Pour boiling water halfway up the basin and cover and steam for 2 hours. Whichever method of steaming you use, check the water level every now and then and top up with boiling water from the kettle, if needed.

5   To serve, turn the pudding out onto a warm plate and serve with the custard.

Per serving: 2360kJ/564kcal (28%), 27.8g fat (40%), 15.7g saturates (79%), 48.5g sugars (54%), 0.39g salt (7%)

MAKES 4
PREP TIME
30 mins, plus
cooling and setting
COOK TIME 50 mins

Custard tarts

These lovely tarts are topped with frosted cranberries and redcurrants

375g pack ready-rolled shortcrust pastry
2 medium eggs, plus 1 egg yolk
40g caster sugar
200ml single cream
75ml whole milk
1 fresh bay leaf
1 tsp freshly grated nutmeg, plus extra

FOR THE FROSTED FRUITS
75g fresh cranberries
75g fresh redcurrants
1 egg white, lightly beaten
50g caster sugar

1   Remove the pastry from the fridge 30 mins before you want to use it.
    Unroll it and use it to line 4 x 10cm fluted tart tins. Put the tins in the fridge
    to chill the pastry for 30 mins.

2   Preheat the oven to 200ºC, fan 180ºC, gas 6. In a heatproof bowl, whisk together
    the eggs and sugar and set aside. Line the pastry cases with baking paper, fill
    with baking beans and blind bake for 15 mins. Remove the beans and baking
    paper and bake for 10 mins. Remove from the oven and cool slightly.

3   Meanwhile, put the cream, milk, bay leaf and nutmeg in a small pan and slowly
    bring to a simmer. Remove the bay leaf from the hot cream, then slowly pour it
    over the egg mixture, stirring constantly. Let the mixture cool slightly, then
    transfer to a jug. Pour the custard mixture into the baked cases, being careful not
    to fill them right to the top as the custard will rise a little as it cooks. Dust over
    the extra nutmeg.

4   Put the tarts on a baking sheet and bake on the middle shelf for 15 mins. Reduce
    the oven temperature to 180ºC, fan 160ºC, gas 5 and bake for a further 10 mins,
    until the custard filling is just starting to brown, but still has a slight wobble at the
    centre. Remove from the oven and transfer to a wire rack. Leave to cool slightly
    in the tins, then remove from the tins to cool completely.

5   While the tarts are cooling, make the frosted fruits. Dip the cranberries and
    redcurrants in the egg white, then roll in the caster sugar to coat. Transfer to a
    tray lined with baking paper and set aside until dry. Top the cooled tarts with
    the frosted cranberries and redcurrants before serving.

Per tart: 2082kJ/499kcal (25%), 30g fat (43%), 15.3g saturates (77%),
27g sugars (30%), 0.47g salt (8%)

SERVES 8
PREP TIME
30 mins, plus cooling
COOK TIME 5 mins

Fig & Marsala trifle

An impressive and indulgent version of a trifle that looks spectacular but couldn't be easier to assemble

200ml Marsala

25g caster sugar

1 tbsp toasted flaked almonds

2 tsp icing sugar

150g ready-made Madeira cake, cubed

75g Taste the Difference soft amaretti, crumbled

8 ripe fresh figs

3 clementines, zested

350g fresh custard by Sainsbury's

300ml fresh double cream

1 Heat the Marsala and caster sugar together in a small pan, until the sugar dissolves. Simmer for 1 min, then pour into a heatproof bowl and leave to cool.

2 Scatter the flaked almonds over a baking sheet, dust with the icing sugar and place under a medium-hot grill for a few seconds, until the sugar starts to caramelise and turn golden.

3 Put the Madeira cake in the base of a 1.5-litre trifle bowl, and scatter over the amaretti. Spoon over 6 tbsp of the Marsala syrup and leave to soak for 5-10 mins.

4 Cut the 'cheeks' from the figs so that you have 16 'cheeks' and 8 thick fig slices. Cut 6 of the 'cheeks' in half to make wedges and finely chop the rest. Thinly cut the segments of 2 clementines into thick rounds and finely chop the remainder.

5 Arrange the thick fig slices and some of the clementine discs around the inside of the trifle bowl. Place all the chopped fruit in the centre, on top of the soaked sponge. Spoon over another 3 tbsp of the syrup. Gently spoon over the custard.

6 Pour the cream into a bowl and whip to soft peaks, then whisk in the remaining Marsala syrup. Spoon the Marsala cream on top of the custard.

7 Decorate with the reserved fig wedges, the clementine zest and caramelised flaked almonds.

Per serving: 2008kJ/481kcal (24%), 26.7g fat (38%), 15g saturates (75%), 42g sugars (47%), 0.15g salt (3%)

Chocolate soufflés

Gooey, rich and moist, these show-stopping puds promise an impressive end to any meal

100g bar Taste the Difference Belgian dark chocolate (72% cocoa solids) with candied orange, broken into squares
A little unsalted butter for greasing

25g caster sugar
3 large eggs, separated
Icing sugar, for dusting
150ml single cream

1   Preheat the oven to 190°C, fan 170°C, gas 5. Put the chocolate in a large heatproof bowl and place over a pan of simmering water, taking care not to let the base of the bowl touch the water. Leave until melted and smooth, then remove from the heat and set aside to cool slightly.

2   Meanwhile, grease 4 x 150ml ramekins with the butter and dust with 2 tsp of the caster sugar. Put the dishes on a baking tray.

3   In a clean, grease-free bowl whisk the egg whites with an electric hand whisk, until stiff. Whisk in the remaining caster sugar, 1 tsp at a time.

4   Beat the egg yolks into the melted chocolate, then stir in a spoonful of the whisked egg white to loosen the mixture. Fold in the remaining egg white until just combined, then spoon into the ramekins. Bake for 10 mins, until risen and just set.

5   To serve, dust the soufflés with icing sugar, make a hole in the centre of each with a teaspoon and fill with a spoonful of the cream.

Per serving: 1296kJ/312kcal (16%), 21.8g fat (31%), 12.6g saturates (63%), 19.4g sugars (22%), 0.2g salt (3%)

Cook's tip
Adding the cream will deflate the soufflé so if you're after the wow factor of a risen soufflé, whip some double cream and serve on the side instead.

Index

Lamb

Lamb & aubergine bake	128
Lamb & chickpea soup	18
Lamb pastitsio	44
Lamb shank, red wine & butterbean stew	124
Lamb shoulder with boulangère potatoes	158
Lamb with tamarind & dates	130
Moroccan-style pot roast leg of lamb	126
Mushroom & pine nut stuffed leg of lamb	160
One-pot lamb with olives & spinach	82
Ras el hanout lamb with tabbouleh	80
Leek, chicken & pearl barley soup	10

Lentils

Lentil cottage pie	136
Pan-fried trout with vegetable & lentil ragù	86
Pancetta, rosemary & red lentil soup	14
Liver & bacon with creamy mash	72

Marsala veal with vegetable remoulade	98

Mash

Chicken chasseur with vegetable mash	68
Creamy cauliflower mash	164
Liver & bacon with creamy mash	72
Roasted garlic mash	38
Melba toasts	22
Mini panettones	166

Monkfish

Monkfish in Parma ham with warm tomato salsa	164
Moroccan-style pot roast leg of lamb	126
Mulligatawny	16

Mushroom

Steak & mushroom Guinness pie	42
Mushroom & pine nut stuffed leg of lamb	160

Mussels

Spaghetti with mussels and cockles	88

Oats

Apple, elderflower & oat crumble	176

Olives

One-pot lamb with olives & spinach	82
Pollock, black olive & preserved lemon tagine	84
One-pot lamb with olives & spinach	82

Oranges

Steamed blood orange pudding	182

Pan-fried duck with herb & orange stuffing	66
Pan-fried trout with vegetable & lentil ragù	86

Pancetta

Pancetta, rosemary & red lentil soup	14
Parkin	148

Parsnip

Spiced parsnip soup with chestnuts	24

Pearl barley

Chicken & squash barley risotto	64
Leek, chicken & pearl barley soup	10
Root vegetable bake	134

Pears

Chocolate & pear cake	168
Roast pears with cardamom butter	174
Peppered roast beef	156

Pies

Bacon lattice pie	38
Chicken, ham & mustard pot pies	32
Cumberland pie	40
Freeform plum & blueberry pie	178
Game pie	58
Irish stew pie	46
Pumpkin pie	150
Steak & mushroom Guinness pie	42

Plums

Confit of duck with spiced plum compote	108
Freeform plum & blueberry pie	178
Pollock, black olive & preserved lemon tagine	84

Pork

Bonfire sausage stew	142
Pork & prune stuffing	152
Pork & winter vegetable stir-fry	78
Sausage, pork & mixed bean stew	112
Slow-roast fennel & coriander pork belly	110
Sticky braised pork ribs with winter slaw	114

Potatoes

Bacon baked potatoes	142
Borscht	26
Ham & potato soup	12
Lamb shoulder with boulangère potatoes	158
Sautéed garlic potatoes	76

Prunes

Pork & prune stuffing	152
Pumpkin pie	150
Purple sprouting broccoli with herb butter	36

Ras el hanout lamb with tabbouleh	80
Red onion & goats' cheese tart	138
Rib-eye steak with Stilton & hollandaise	76

Risotto

Chicken & squash barley risotto	64
Risotto-stuffed mini squash	144

Roast chicken with winter root vegetables	30
Roast pears with cardamom butter	174
Roasted garlic mash	38
Roasted stuffed goose	152
Root vegetable bake	134

Salad

Winter salad	120

Salmon

Baby leaf spinach soup with salmon	22
Classic fish soup	20
Side of salmon with horseradish crust	162

Sausage

Bonfire sausage stew	142
Sausage, pork & mixed bean stew	112
Sautéed garlic potatoes	76
Sautéed kale with hazelnuts	70
Savoury drop scones	8

Seafood/Shellfish

Classic fish soup	20
Spaghetti with mussels and cockles	88
Squid & chorizo casserole	132
Side of salmon with horseradish crust	162
Slow-roast fennel & coriander pork belly	110
Spaghetti with mussels and cockles	88
Speedy chicken broth	8
Spiced parsnip soup with chestnuts	24
Spicy shredded beef	120

Spinach

Baby leaf spinach soup with salmon	22
One-pot lamb with olives & spinach	82

Squash

Chicken & squash barley risotto	64
Pumpkin pie	150
Risotto-stuffed mini squash	144
Squid & chorizo casserole	132
Steak & mushroom Guinness pie	42
Steamed blood orange pudding	182

Stews

Bonfire sausage stew	142
Catalan bean stew	90
Irish stew pie	46
Italian-style veg stew	92
Lamb shank, red wine & butterbean stew	124
Sausage, pork & mixed bean stew	112
Sticky braised pork ribs with winter slaw	114

Stilton

Rib-eye steak with Stilton & hollandaise	76

Stir-fry

Pork & winter vegetable stir-fry	78

Tabbouleh

Ras el hanout lamb with tabbouleh	80

Index

Conversion table

Weights		Volume		Measurements		Oven temperatures		
							fan	gas
15g	½ oz	25ml	1fl oz	2mm	¹⁄₁₆ in	110°C	90°C	
25g	1 oz	50ml	2fl oz	3mm	⅛ in	120°C	100°C	½
40g	1½ oz	75ml	3fl oz	4mm	¹⁄₆ in	140°C	120°C	1
50g	2 oz	100ml	4fl oz	5mm	¼ in	150°C	130°C	2
60g	2½ oz	150ml	5fl oz (¼ pint)	1cm	½ in	160°C	140°C	3
75g	3 oz	175ml	6fl oz	2cm	¾ in	180°C	160°C	4
100g	3½ oz	200ml	7fl oz	2.5cm	1 in	190°C	170°C	5
125g	4 oz	225ml	8fl oz	3cm	1¼ in	200°C	180°C	6
150g	5 oz	250ml	9fl oz	4cm	1½ in	220°C	200°C	7
175g	6 oz	300ml	10fl oz (½ pint)	4.5cm	1¾ in	230°C	210°C	8
200g	7 oz	350ml	13fl oz	5cm	2 in	240°C	220°C	9
225g	8 oz	400ml	14fl oz	6cm	2½ in			
250g	9 oz	450ml	16fl oz (¾ pint)	7.5cm	3 in			
275g	10 oz	600ml	20fl oz (1 pint)	9cm	3½ in			
300g	11 oz	750ml	25fl oz (1¼ pints)	10cm	4 in			
350g	12 oz	900ml	30fl oz (1½ pints)	13cm	5 in			
375g	13 oz	1 litre	34fl oz (1¾ pints)	13.5cm	5¼ in			
400g	14 oz	1.2 litres	40fl oz (2 pints)	15cm	6 in			
425g	15 oz	1.5 litres	52fl oz (2½ pints)	16cm	6½ in			
450g	1 lb	1.8 litres	60fl oz (3 pints)	18cm	7 in			
500g	1 lb 2 oz			19cm	7½ in			
650g	1 lb 7 oz			20cm	8 in			
675g	1½ lb			23cm	9 in			
700g	1 lb 9 oz			24cm	9½ in			
750g	1 lb 11 oz			25.5cm	10 in			
900g	2 lb			28cm	11 in			
1kg	2 lb 4 oz			30cm	12 in			
1.5kg	3 lb 6 oz			32.5cm	13 in			
				35cm	14 in			

Sainsbury's food safety advice

General kitchen safety guidelines

- Remember to wash your hands thoroughly before food preparation. If handling raw meat, fish or poultry, it's equally important to wash your hands after preparation, too.
- Keep raw food separate from ready-to-eat foods when you're preparing meals; use separate chopping boards and utensils or wash thoroughly between use.
- Washing raw poultry spreads bacteria around the kitchen via tiny splashes, which increases the risk of cross-contamination to other foods. The best way to destroy harmful bacteria is by cooking thoroughly, until piping hot throughout with no pink colour remaining in the flesh.
- Refer to ingredient packaging for full preparation and cooking instructions.

- Public health advice is to avoid consumption of raw or lightly cooked eggs, especially for those vulnerable to infections, including pregnant women, babies and the elderly.
- Wash fresh vegetables, fruit and herbs (including any used for garnishing dishes) before use.
- When reheating leftovers, make sure they are piping hot throughout.

Freezing and defrosting

- Products can be frozen up to use-by dates (check labels to see if suitable to freeze).
- Defrost food overnight in the fridge (covered in a dish to avoid contaminating other products).

Refrigerating food

- Keep your fridge temperature below 5°C.
- To avoid cross-contamination, cover raw meat and poultry and store at the bottom of the fridge, separate from ready-to-eat food.
- When preparing food, keep out of the fridge for the shortest time possible.
- Cool down leftovers as quickly as possible then, once cooled, cover, put in the fridge and eat within two days.
- Clean your fridge regularly to ensure it remains hygienic and in good working condition.
- For tinned food, decant the contents into a non-metallic container and seal.

'Best before' and 'use-by' dates

- Food with a 'use-by' date goes off quite quickly and could pose a health risk if consumed after this date.
- Food with a 'best before' date is longer-lasting. It is safe to eat after this date but will not be at its best quality.

Recipe nutrition

The nutrition information on each recipe shown in this book has been calculated using Sainsbury's own-brand products and is based on 1 adult portion, assuming equal division of the recipe into the suggested number of servings.

Nutrition is calculated using each recipe's ingredients list only and does not include any sides, accompaniments or other serving suggestions mentioned in the method unless otherwise stated. The nutrition content will vary if other products are used or if the servings are not identical. Also, variations in cooking methods may affect the nutrition content.

The nutritional information on each recipe also includes the percentage of Reference Intakes (RIs) provided by a serving. RIs are a guide to the maximum amounts of calories, fat, saturates, sugars and salt an adult should consume in a day (based on an average female adult) and are as follows:

Energy or nutrient	Reference Intake per day
Energy	8400kJ/2000kcal
Total fat	70g
Saturates	20g
Total sugars	90g
Salt	6g

Seasoning: we're committed to promoting healthier eating and lowering salt in daily diets. As such we have worked hard to produce recipes that do not need as much (if any) salt seasoning. Note: recipe nutrition does not include any salt you add yourself.

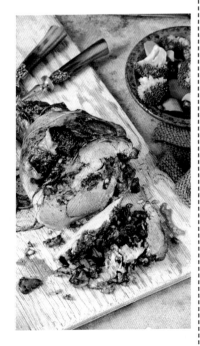

For more information on food safety and nutrition, visit sainsburys.co.uk/livewellforless and sainsburys.co.uk/kitchensafety

Traditional food that made Britain Great...

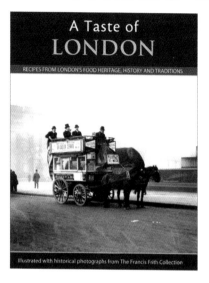

The Francis Frith Collection © as seen on TV

REGIONAL RECIPE BOOKS FROM AROUND BRITAIN

Discover the delicious variety of Britain's traditional dishes and produce, as well as some of the stories and fascinating facts behind the recipes. A journey given added flavour by the delightful period photographs from the world-famous Francis Frith Collection, showing the people and places of Britain's past.

Titles include: Scotland, The North-West, The North-East, Yorkshire, West Midlands, East Midlands, Wales, Lincolnshire & the Fens, East Anglia, Gloucestershire & the Cotswolds, The South-West, The Thames Valley, London, The South-East.*

Other ranges available from selected Sainsbury's stores:

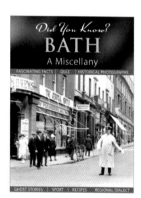

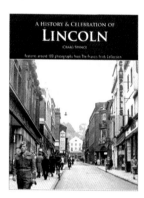

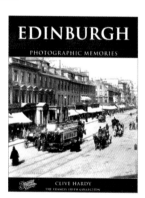

90 books each focused on a specific town or area and containing fascinating facts, local dialect and phrases, ghost stories, traditional recipes, sporting trivia and a quiz. Illustrated with historical photographs from The Francis Frith Collection these books make a fabulous gift, or souvenir.

A series of 50 books, each celebrating a town, or city – its history and development right up to the 20th century. Including stories about local events and personalities, plus photographs from The Francis Frith Collection supplemented with contemporary images. Exclusive to Sainsbury's – every book contains a voucher for a free mounted print.

Journey back in time with these 55 books – each providing a pictorial history of a town or region. Lavishly illustrated with evocative photographs from The Francis Frith Collection and texts written by local authors. Exclusive to Sainsbury's – every book contains a voucher for a free mounted print.

THE FRANCIS FRITH COLLECTION© Photographic publishers since 1860

www.francisfrith.com

Credits

Food
Food editor Angela Romeo
Assistant food editor Lottie Covell
Food assistant Nadine Brown
Recipes & food styling
Val Barret, Angela Drake, Emma Franklin,
Kat Mead, Nichola Palmer, Mima Sinclair,
Joy Skipper, Hannah Yeadon

Editorial
Head of content Helen Renshaw
Editor Christine Faughlin
Sub editor Ward Hellewell

Design & photography
Head of design Scott McKenzie
Art director Dan Perry
Prop stylist Morag Farquhar
Photography Lara Holmes
Sainsbury's magazine **photography**
Peter Cassidy, Dan Jones, Martin Poole,
Kate Whitaker
Sainsbury's magazine **recipes**
Emma Franklin, Ghillie James, Lucy Jessop,
Kat Mead, Sarah Randell
Additional food stylists Angela Boggiano,
Seiko Hatfield, Joss Herd, Bianca Nice,
Sunil Vijayakar
Additional stylists Liz Belton, Iris Bromet,
Claire Hunt, Rachel Jukes, Wei Tang

Account management
Account manager Jo Brennan
Client director Andy Roughton

For Sainsbury's
Book team Phil Carroll, Lynne de Lacy,
Robyn Haque, Tony Jagpal, Mavis Sarfo,
Nutrition Alastair McArthur
Product safety manager Nikki Mosley

Production
Production director Sophie Dillon
Colour origination F1 Colour Ltd

Special thanks to...
Sophie Banda, Francesca Clarke, Frances
Ewings, Jenna Leiter, Marcus Ludewig,
Pam Price, Julie Stevens, Sasha Turnbull

seven.co.uk

Sainsbury's magazine

* Delicious triple-tested recipes your family will love

* Interesting and inspiring features

* Great fashion and beauty ideas

* Tempting offers and exciting competitions

LOVE ALL THIS AND WANT MORE?

If you subscribe to *Sainsbury's magazine* you'll get it delivered straight to your door before it hits the shops and benefit from exclusive gifts and offers, too! Visit **sainsburysmagazine.co.uk** for our latest great-value subscription offer

MIX
Paper from
responsible sources
FSC® C005461
www.fsc.org